MW01520117

THE ESSENTIAL PROBLEM SOLVER
A SIX-STEP METHOD FOR CREATING SOLUTIONS THAT LAST

Copyright 2020
Bill Straubinger

Published by:
Results for Change Publishing
www.resultsforchange.org

Editing by:
Margaret Daisley
Blue Horizon Books
www.bluehorizonbooks.com

Cover and design by:
Dawn Daisley
MorningliteBookDesign
www.morninglitebookdesign.com

Publisher's Cataloging-in-Publication data:
Straubinger, Bill
The Essential Problem Solver
ISBN: 978-1-7352156-0-0

The Essential PROBLEM SOLVER

A SIX-STEP METHOD FOR CREATING SOLUTIONS THAT LAST

BILL STRAUBINGER

Contents

"You can't stop the waves
but you can learn to surf."

— Jon Kabat-Zinn

Introduction

Have there been times when you've come up with a solution to a problem at work, only to find you've been dealing with the wrong issue? Is there a problem that you or others in your organization have avoided moving forward to solve, simply because you don't know how to solve it?

What's the cost of not being able to solve the problem? Does it affect the company's bottom line or the budget for your department? Will it affect your ability to get that next promotion?

Unfortunately, many times we address only the symptoms of the problem and not the real issue—because it's easier and we're looking for the quick fix. We may not even understand what the real problem is, much less have a process for figuring out how to solve the problem

Obviously, some problems are more important and urgent than others. Some might have a deadline or a budget that has to be met, with consequences involving the whole company. Other problems might be as straightforward as deciding what to order for a group's lunch-time meeting.

This book is about solving problems at work, but the Six Steps to Problem Solving are also effective at home or in other organizations where groups of people need to work together to achieve satisfactory outcomes.

Why do we need to learn effective tools for problem solving?

In the workplace, acquiring strong problem-solving expertise is essential for managers, but it's also very important for employees, especially those involved in working on teams or committees. In the current fast-changing global economy, employers often identify everyday problem-solving skills as vital to the success of their organizations. For employees, problem solving can be used to develop practical and creative solutions, and to show independence and initiative to supervisors.

In short, being able to demonstrate an ability to effectively solve problems in the workplace can make the difference between achieving your employer's goals, or not, and being considered for a promotion, or not.

Some of the key problem-solving skills organizations are seeking include an ability to identify and implement measures to:

- increase productivity,

- improve efficiency,

- develop new products,

- enhance customer service.

Problem-solving skills are critical in all those areas, and they are also crucial in conducting negotiations and achieving effective conflict resolutions.

WHO NEEDS TO LEARN ESSENTIAL PROBLEM-SOLVING SKILLS?

Since we all have to solve problems inside and outside of the workplace, it's important to learn these critical skills, no matter what your role is. Whether the issues are big or small, we all face situations and challenges that we have to deal with and make decisions about—decisions that will affect us in the future.

Sometimes, it is simply up to us as individuals to solve the problem, as quickly and efficiently as possible, given the resources at our disposal at the time.

However, it is more likely in the workplace that resolving a problem requires the collaboration of different team members. Maybe these team members are in the same building and work on the same project you're working on, or maybe they work in different locations, or even in another organization. The team could involve people who are all part of the same department and share many of the same experiences and ideas, but it is more likely that your team is made up of people from many different organizational levels, and many different areas of expertise, backgrounds, styles, life experiences and perspectives.

So, the key question when it comes to problem solving is how can we effectively and efficiently engage with other team members, so that we are all part of the solution. How can we avoid creating extra problems, and focus on truly creating solutions that last?

Our methods will give everybody on the team a chance to be heard and understood. As you move through the model, it will also afford you the time to reflect and ruminate before coming up with a solution.

In the end, it will provide a vehicle to give everyone on a team an opportunity to contribute, buy in and know exactly what the next steps are and their role in accomplishing the plan.

THE SIX STEPS TO PROBLEM SOLVING

On the following page is a diagram that outlines the six essential steps to problem solving. As we move through the various steps in this book, we'll highlight each step one at a time, and focus on the processes involved in that particular step.

As you will see, one of the most important steps is to consider other points of view in helping to truly understand and address a problem. Having many different frames of reference gives us the most accurate and complete understanding of both problems and solutions. Having an awareness of these multiple points of view is a key to finding the best possible and/or most effective solutions.

In fact, the most important message of this book is to simply Stop & Think! We all have a tendency to fall back on what we call Automatic Thinking—making assumptions that may have very little bearing on the situation at hand, and which many times doesn't provide much help in solving the problem.

As we move towards generating possible solutions to a problem, brainstorming plays a critical role. It's what many call "thinking outside the box." Brainstorming is frequently done in conjunction with others, for instance a team or committee, with the idea of generating as many different ideas as possible in a given amount of time.

After assessing the impact of alternative solutions, the next step is to select an option or options and then create an implementation plan. The plan should include identifying and using available resources, while considering barriers and obstacles to success. It will also include assigning roles, setting deadlines, expected outcomes and how to anticipate and deal with possible obstacles.

By defining aspects of the implementation plan you will have already established some reliable methods for being able to later effectively review and evaluate progress solving the problem. We also need to be able to capture what we've learned, which is the final step in the essential problem-solving process.

However, if you're not satisfied with the initial outcomes of your solution, you'll also be able to recalibrate as necessary, and even go back to a previous step. For instance, you may need to collect more information about the new way you're looking at the problem and/or you may need to re-define the problem itself.

STEP 1. DEVELOP AWARENESS (INVESTIGATE)

Awareness of your own assumptions and feelings about problems—and others' assumptions and feelings as well—is a key to effectively understand exactly what the problem is. Ask those who have information about the problem to explain the important elements. Have others who are participating in solving the problem ask key questions of team members so that they can get the needed data and share their experiences. Getting team members to share their knowledge and feelings about the problem will help to further understand the issue.

There will be times when you have to rely on yourself alone to solve a problem. Perhaps there is a deadline looming and no time to consult with others. Maybe you feel it's a small matter that doesn't really need a group to solve.

More likely, though, you will be working as part of a team, whether on-site or virtual, made up of people with similar and different levels of expertise, skills, styles, beliefs, and of course problem-solving skills. However, even if you are the only decision-maker in the problem-solving process, it is imperative that you examine your assumptions about the problem and where those assumptions come from. You need to also become acutely aware of your own approach to identifying the problem and defining solutions.

It is just as important also for you to make yourself aware of the presumptions of each and every team member involved in the process. You need to also become aware of the reality of their experiences, beliefs and points of view, as these are going to directly affect the process of defining the problem and coming up with solutions.

Stop & Think is the most important part of the Six Step process, though it is not actually one of the steps. It is the moment when you decide how you're going to define and explore aspects of the problem. Should you be trying to work on this by yourself, or do you involve others in the problem-solving process?

Most likely you will be working with people on your team, people in the organization who are somehow affected by the problem and/or therefore might be involved in solving it. It is just as important at this stage to become aware of the problem-solving skills of others on your team, as it is to examine your own thinking skills and assumptions. You could say that this important step is about "thinking about thinking."

When you work with a group of people, the process of defining a problem and identifying solutions is interactive. Effective interaction with a team depends on being open to and aware of others' perspectives, as well as being able to clearly communicate your own ideas and feelings. These skills are covered in the next steps, but it begins with an awareness of how you and your team members approach the particular problem and problem solving in general.

STEP 2. DEFINE THE PROBLEM (DETERMINE)

Defining the problem—it sounds so simple, doesn't it? And yet identifying the right problem is often difficult, as the process itself can be loaded with problems. For instance, if you are only identifying symptoms of the problem, the problem won't be solved. And if you make assumptions about the problem that aren't accurate—for instance, based on similar problems you've encountered in the past, but which aren't totally relevant to the current situation—your solution may be doomed from the start.

Still, you know there is a problem, otherwise you wouldn't be looking to solve it. You can see the problem—for instance, in sales numbers that are off—or hear about it from people you work with or unhappy customers. This is the point where you might get others involved, where you can collect information and feedback about what they think or feel the problem is. Ask good questions, of yourself and others, to be sure you understand all the intricacies of the issue you're dealing with.

In the end, you should try to define your problem as an open-ended question, which will jump-start your thinking. As you begin answering that open-ended question, it will help you to more accurately solve the real problem.

STEP 3. EXPLORE THE PROBLEM (EXAMINE)

In using the Thinking It Through process, you will develop an awareness about your issue, situation or challenge, and formulate the right questions to ask. Through further investigation, you will collect the necessary information, clarify its authenticity and relevance, then confirm and verify what you believe is true. The final element in this part of the process is to consider other points of view. This can be gathered by getting multiple perspectives from others involved in the problem.

We need to be able to take the time to thoughtfully review all the data we've gathered through reflection. Using Inclusive/Reflective thinking will give us the ability to appreciate, comprehend and welcome the full picture and deal effectively with all the different perspectives of the situation we face. Our minds need to be open to new ideas and information and alternative ways of viewing the issue.

To be an Essential Problem Solver, you need to make sure you're focusing your mind on all the necessary information coming from all the key players involved, assessing the value of that information, and reflecting on it in light of previously gathered thoughts, ideas and data.

STEP 4. GENERATE, ANALYZE AND SELECT OPTIONS (EXPAND & DECIDE)

In this step, you get to generate and evaluate options for solving the problem. Both inclusive and reflective thinking processes can be used, whether you are working by yourself or with others.

How can we expand our choices? One technique to help us uncover new options is brainstorming. There are two key guidelines for success in brainstorming—brainstorm without criticism, and use possibility thinking.

When sorting, ranking, developing, and choosing options generated in a brainstorming session, we need to be deliberate and explicit in creating choice criteria. Setting measurements for success will help us think more clearly and constructively about the factors that will influence the eventual success or failure of our efforts.

The real first steps towards defining the solutions to the problem must be carefully considered. For instance, do we need research? Should we involve other people? If so, when, where, and how do we do that? Most likely you are going to have to rely on others in your organization to help implement solutions you've decided on, and because of that, you will need to involve others in the process of defining the solution, as well as executing the plan.

STEP 5. IMPLEMENT SOLUTIONS (TAKE ACTION)

The next step is to create an implementation plan that specifies the tasks that need to be done and time frames for work to be completed or reports assembled.

Finally, we need to be specific about who else needs to be involved in implementing the plan. Do you need to recruit them first, or are they already on board? Once involved in the implementation plan, they will need to know what they are expected to do, and when they are expected to do it.

STEP 6. REVIEW AND ASSESS PROGRESS (EVALUATE)

How do you know if your solution is working? You will need to include in the plan a process for reviewing your solution, measuring it, assessing it, and getting feedback from those affected. You might build a review date into the process, or it might arise naturally, for instance if approval is needed for funding, or if sales results are tied to quarterly reports.

If a natural date is not apparent, a specific date should be set to review progress. This needs to be done early in the process to be sure any problems can be identified, and course corrections can be planned and implemented. It is also important to create ways to capture what we learn as the plan proceeds.

"We are what we repeatedly do."

—Aristotle

Real Life Examples

T hroughout the book, we'll be using business story examples to provide scenarios where the elements of the Six Steps apply. In a team-driven environment exploring situations—especially in groups of people with different styles, areas of expertise, experience and agendas—our approach will be extremely useful.

The key player in these examples is a fictional manager, Paul Moore, described on the following pages. Anytime you see his picture, it will denote we're using Paul's story. By using Paul's specific business experiences with other employees, we'll come into contact with the many problems and challenges he faces and how employees struggle to deal with them and come up with great solutions, together and separately. We think you'll recognize some of these problems and challenges as being very similar to ones you've experienced yourself.

In addition, we end each chapter with questions to help you think about how the information in that particular step applies to your own real-life situations.

We can't guarantee that these processes will solve every one of your problems. We can promise, however, that the six-step problem-solving method will provide a clear way to identify your issues, and give you tools to help explore key elements, provide a process to creatively come up with solutions, guide you in establishing a plan to test your ideas and then evaluate your project's success and, if necessary, remap your plan.

As you monitor your plan's progress, if you feel it is not moving forward, you can re-engage with the Thinking it Through Process to develop awareness about why it's not working, then move down through the other steps to re-evaluate aspects of your plan, generate new options, or make course corrections.

Let's be clear—we can give you the tools, but only you can put in the hard work of applying the elements of the model. And, as many people have already learned, problem solving becomes easier when you know how to approach it skillfully.

What we can guarantee is that when you use this six-step method, you'll have taken the critical first step in finding the best solutions to your problems, ones that will last.

PAUL'S STORY

Meet Paul Moore, a 43-year-old father of two teenagers—Billy, who is a high school sophomore, and Karen, who is graduating from high school this June. Paul has been married to Betty for 20 years.

Paul commutes more than an hour daily from his home in New Rochelle to his job in New York City. There, he is a Vice President of Regional Accounts for Energize, a mid-sized U.S. retail chain that specializes in healthy foods at a reasonable price. He supervises ten employees, mostly managers and administrative types, and is responsible for the success of twelve stores located primarily in the southeastern United States. He travels approximately thirty percent of the time, visiting the stores in his region, but would rather spend less time on the road.

Working in the food industry for over twenty years, Paul worked his way up from clerk to store manager with a major supermarket chain before joining Energize, when it started up fifteen years ago. Energize has had a meteoric rise over the last five years and currently has 75 stores around the country specializing in both organic and non-organic varieties of healthy foods. Paul has also had a rapid rise through the Energize ranks and is now one of the youngest VPs in the company. Paul cares a great deal about his own personal development and that of the people he supervises, organizing various training opportunities throughout the year. Paul feels he's been successful in his current position at Energize by keeping his region in the top two in sales over the last four years. He has also developed many new programs which have improved employee morale and retention in his department.

Recently, two of Paul's regional managers, Tom and Mike, were laid off due to reorganization. Although Paul and his other six managers knew this layoff made perfect business sense, three of the other managers were very concerned and upset about what had happened to their colleagues. "Thinking from a dollars and cents business perspective is only part of the picture," Diane, one of the managers, told him. She also felt that Tom and Mike were not being treated fairly because no explicit reasons were ever given for letting them go. Even worse, she feared that she could be next.

In this case, employee unhappiness and misconceptions happened because no one had taken the time to speak with the managers about Energize's current and future business plans.

Paul knew that this could present an even more unsettling long-term problem concerning the managers' projections regarding other possible future business changes. He also realized that it might negatively affect their subsequent interactions with others—customers, suppliers, etc.—in how they represented the company to them.

Paul decided it was important for him to spend more time with all his staff to understand their feelings and concerns. He knew it wasn't enough that they understood the logic of the company's decisions, but what they believed would be true in the future as a result of those choices and the fear that they might be next. It would also give him the opportunity to more fully explain the company's rationale for the tough business decisions that might be coming down the pike. So, Paul decided to hold monthly staff meetings focused on dispersing information and soliciting feedback about what's going on in the company.

In this situation, Paul relied on his own skill set and experiences to handle the problem and come up with solutions. He had taken a variety of business courses over the years to improve his management and leadership skills. He also encourages his managers to take courses, and uses various instruments that he's familiar with, like thinking and behavioral style assessments, which assess a person's strengths and weaknesses.

Paul's management style creates a common language among the employees he supervises. It also helps him and his team understand similarities and differences. For instance, some of the staff are more big picture thinkers and some are more detail-oriented thinkers. Some are more directed by logic, and some are focused on emotions in how they see and interact with the world.

Paul knows that it's important that other employees recognize and understand this information, because they can then focus on trying to build upon their strengths, while being aware of and working on their limitations. When they do this, Paul knows that it will give these employees a better understanding of how they can work best together.

Paul also knows his own personal strong points. When it came to pitching the new "customer referral program," he used his enthusiasm and emphasis on how people feel to help get everyone excited and wanting to play a part in making it successful. It worked, for the most part. A large majority of his department's employees signed up after he made his presentation.

Paul has learned to also recognize his shortcomings, like not paying enough attention to detail. As an example, Paul recently had his department switch to a new financial software package to track customer accounts. He truly didn't understand the full ramifications of what information was needed and why.

The adverse result was Paul had to go back and have Marta, his administrative assistant, take another four hours to correct some of the errors, when she could have been working on the new marketing plan. The problem occurred because all the data wasn't inputted correctly, since Paul thought that certain information wasn't important to the project.

ORGANIZATIONAL CHART FOR PAUL AND HIS REPORTS

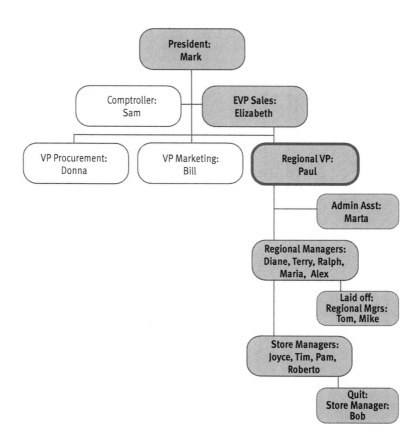

Step 1.
Develop Awareness

The first part of this section helps you take a good look at yourself. We explore the way your physical, social, and emotional lives are set up, and how they interact to impact your problem-solving skills. An awareness of yourself—thinking and understanding about how you see yourself and how you live in the world—is critical to becoming an essential problem solver.

It's not just a matter of introspection; it's a matter of exploring how others see us, by getting useful and appropriate feedback. This forms the bedrock of how you see, approach, and interact with others as you gather and process the information used in creating solutions to your problems.

How do I know who I am?

Look in the mirror and what do I see?

A familiar face or a stranger
staring back at me?

IT ALL STARTS WITH Y.O.U.

Y.O.U. means Your Own Understanding of yourself. Gaining knowledge about yourself is an important initial step in becoming aware of "who you are" and what you know. The more you know about YOU, the more you'll understand your SELF—your values, beliefs, feelings and the many preferences and limitations you have for behaving, learning, thinking, taking in and processing information, as well as how you work with other people.

When you understand where your perspective or point of view comes from, you'll have an opportunity to see how you are similar and different from the other people you interact with in life. If you take a moment to reflect on where you're coming from, it helps you to understand how this affects your thoughts, emotions, ideas, aspirations, beliefs and/or actions related to any topic or person you're interacting with, as well as how you approach problem solving.

Paul's interest in self-development started in college when he majored in psychology and continued through his participation in group and individual workshops over the years. He has attended these sessions through the businesses he's worked for and on his own, for personal growth.

Through these activities, he has learned a lot about himself and developed a healthy appreciation of others. He also knows that unless he has a good understanding of himself–his strengths, weaknesses, and personality–he won't be able to truly value, interact with, or bring out the best in others on his team.

KNOWLEDGE OF SELF LEADS TO KNOWLEDGE OF OTHERS

As you apply the following principles to understanding yourself, you will see how they apply to understanding others—your employees and/or team members. If you don't understand, for instance, how to be a good observer, you can't expect others on your team to be good observers, and you can't teach them how to become good observers.

BECOME A GOOD OBSERVER

An important element in knowing ourselves is being a good observer—to accurately understand and evaluate how we are perceiving what we see and how we are seen by others.

How do we become good observers? Take a moment to step back to look at how you and others are viewing your current environment. Seriously, stop and look around you, and make an assessment. It's a crucial action toward your gaining an accurate perception of how you and others are seeing the world.

Then, think of a problem or situation you've encountered in your workplace, and ask yourself:

- **How was my point of view and others' points of view about the problem the same, and how did they differ?** Asking the question of ourselves and others about how we know what we know will give you a handle on your perception of situations versus how others are interpreting it. For instance, if we think expanding the business is important to success but others think improving the elements of the existing business will prove to be more effective, it's obvious we have different points of view.

- **How can I see my own perceptions and others' perceptions more clearly?** It's very difficult to take an objective view of your own subjective perceptions, so getting the feedback of others is important for you to be able to clarify how others see you and your interpretations. If we keep proposing expanding the company's offering of organic products and continue getting nowhere, we need to get feedback from others about why they see this differently and have them explain their point of view.

Paul realizes that he and many other employees have a lot of similarities, like wanting to be "successful." The challenge is that Ralph, Diane and Alex, some of his regional managers, have very different definitions of "success." Ralph sees success as getting more power, while for Alex it's making more money, and Diane thinks winning the Employee of the Month award is a marker of success.

Paul also knows that many issues are not simply black and white, like the question that came up at a recent staff meeting on the topic of whether the company should cut down or increase organic foods in the stores.

Paul thought it was important to take a step back and assess what he and the other staff members believed was true. He wanted to be sure to get adequate information and encourage everyone to ask questions to explore all the shades of gray involved with the issue. Diane thought they should listen to what customers had to say and how they felt. Ralph perceived that it was more of a profit and loss decision. The result of the meeting was not a single answer, but a step towards a more nuanced approach.

It was decided that in some of the store's departments, like vegetables, it might be important to offer more organic produce, but in departments such as meat it would definitely be too limiting.

"Also, where the stores were located should play a big part in the decision-making process," added Terry, a new regional manager, who realized their decisions related to another pressing issue, that of buying local products. In the end, Paul realized all of these elements needed to play a critical part in their decision-making and more investigation needed to be done.

Ask yourself:
How do you know that to be true?

PERCEPTION

Perception is reality—or at least our own reality. For example, if a person has the title of vice-president, most people assume he or she is very intelligent. But is that always true?

This is one of the key elements in understanding how we and others know what we know to be "true." The one basic question, you can ask yourself and others is: How do you know that to be true?

We need to have a basic understanding of how our perceptions and others' perceptions are formed, in order to truly have an accurate self-awareness and an awareness of others. Reality is where each of us lives and each of our realities is based on how we create meaning and perceive the world around us.

In other words, different people's perceptions are never exactly the same. We come from different backgrounds, different educational and occupational paths, and we have our own unique personalities. It is only natural that our perception of the world is different than another person's perception of the world.

If we don't ask these questions of ourselves and others, we wind up falling back on using Automatic Thinking—we make decisions without having thought the problem through, and we don't even know what criteria we are using to make these decisions.

Preconceived notions govern our responses unless we work to change them.

Here is an example of a manager making a decision using Automatic Thinking, based on his past experience:

> **Problem:** People are working overtime and the work is still not getting done.
>
> **Assumption:** What do you believe is true? The manager's automatic reaction: *There are not enough people to do the work.*
>
> **Conclusion:** What judgement can I make? The manager's automatic reaction: *We need additional staff.*
>
> **Response:** What do we need to do? The manager's automatic reaction: *I will hire more people.*

Unfortunately, as it turned out, that was the wrong solution. In this example, the manager made presumptions about how to solve the problem based solely on previous experience. Hiring more people because the work wasn't getting done did not work, because as it turned out, there were new factors that he had not considered. This is a classic example of Automatic Thinking. When you encounter a problem that seems familiar, it is natural and necessary to ask yourself what's similar to your past experience, but most importantly, you need to then ask yourself what is different.

If a problem is not solved, we need to explore the reasons why we believed this assumption was true. In this example, the real problem could have been that poor supervision of the existing employees led to them not being able to get the work done. Or it could have been that the employees didn't have the right knowledge about the work or the skills to do it. Or perhaps they just wanted to get more overtime. In other words, the manager needed to ask more questions to find out what the real problem was, in order to find the right solutions.

SAME/DIFFERENT

One of the main dichotomies in our self/other awareness is that we are all the same, and we are all different from each other, simultaneously. We are the same in that we all want to be successful and avoid failing. However, we are different in that how each of us defines "success" and what makes each of us feel successful or unsuccessful is different. "Success" is just one characteristic that is an individual matter that makes us unique.

It's very important to understand that how we see and understand a situation, issue or challenge will always at least slightly be different from how others see it. It may be similar, but not exactly the same. Our interpretations of reality are distinctive.

SIMPLE/COMPLICATED

Also, we are both simple and complicated. We are simple in our commonalities, our inter-dependence and connectedness with each other, but we are complicated in the fact that we're all individuals, independent and separate, with different points of view.

Be aware that focusing only on our similarities may make us miss the unique way we all see things. But focusing only on our differences can divide us, and sometimes sever our connections with each other. In the workplace, the result may be taking positions such as "us versus them," which could negatively affect us in solving the problem.

How each of us understands the world is our own reality. Our individual realities are neither right nor wrong, good or bad, only different. We need to remember that all of these are individual truths and realize that we constantly move back and forth between these same/different and simple/complicated areas. This helps to understand ourselves and others and gives us a more balanced and fluid view of reality, which is helpful when we're using Inclusive/Reflective thinking.

SELECTIVE PERCEPTION

For the most part, we all, instantly, tend to perceive our environment according to our prior beliefs, feelings, knowledge and experiences, and then we react accordingly. For example, seeing someone who is well-dressed, we might treat them with respect, whereas if someone is dressed sloppily, we may not treat them as well.

So, what does changing our perception require and what does that mean?

Let's understand that we all have prejudices, which simply means pre-judgments. But our prejudices may wind up being used as filters/lenses/frames in different aspects of life in how we perceive things. In the workplace, for instance, while one person may view a situation from the perspective of a customer service manager, another person may have the perspective of a marketing or advertising manager, and they are bound to have different experiences and different perceptions of the same problem. Just having an awareness of that fact alone will help us to comprehend our own and others' thinking. Why do I see it this way? Why do others see it their way? How do I know that to be true? Good questions to ask!

Unfortunately, gaining knowledge and experience isn't always the solution. As we get older or become more of an expert in an area, often the result is that it gets harder for us to see other people's points of view. This is especially true if it contradicts our view or doesn't fit into what we believe is true.

Having an open mind and being able to accept that there are different ways of looking at things is a key element in understanding the perception process. Being aware and acknowledging our own perspectives and prejudices and those of others, can also serve as an important first step in trying to keep our minds more open.

 At a recent meeting, Paul's staff discussed how they could offer a wider variety of organic products in their stores. Paul was sure to include not only all members of his department, but also Bill from Marketing. He additionally invited administrative and support representatives from the Sales department, to be sure he got as many diverse opinions as possible.

He was quick to see that most of the support staff remained quiet. They seemed unsure their ideas would be accepted. He subsequently came up with a plan that in the future he would have each person fill out post-it notes with their suggestions, so he could collect input in a way to get everyone's participation anonymously.

The result was that Paul received many good new ideas from the entire group and some from the administrative staff that were ultimately incorporated into the plan.

Paul is not perfect, however. He's made many decisions in which he failed to get others' input before moving forward. For example: he recently changed the monthly reporting procedure without realizing it conflicted with the availability of necessary financial figures. Luckily, it wasn't too difficult for him to acknowledge his mistake and subsequently revise the procedure.

Paul remembers a time when he was a regional manager and was visiting the South Carolina store. As he was casually roaming the store, he noticed a large group of people in the fresh vegetable area. He observed that they were very actively selecting the produce. When he got closer, he overheard a couple of customers remarking about "How great it was that Energize was offering these products," and how they "wished there would be more fresh produce available."

From these perceptions, Paul developed a point of view that fresh vegetables were a real winner for the store, and that they should consider expanding this product area. When Paul mentioned this to Pam, the store manager, he got a totally different point of view. As a matter of fact, Pam and the produce section manager had recently discussed decreasing the fresh vegetable section.

It seemed some customers were increasingly causing a mess by disturbing the displays, eating some of the produce and even dropping produce on the floor, which was causing some waste and safety issues as people would slip while walking through the aisle. Because a lot of the fresh produce was either going bad or being bruised by all the manhandling, it also was becoming a money loser for the store. Paul quickly could see how important it was to get different perceptions, as they can lead to varying points of view and he revised his thinking.

OPEN-MINDEDNESS

To accurately explore our perceptions, we need to be open-minded. We often assume that what we see, think, feel and believe is the only reality there is. This tends to lead us to misinterpret our own view as the truth. This belief in our "knowing" and our assumption that we are "right" becomes easy to maintain when we choose to ignore the faults or errors that might lie in our thinking.

Sometimes our reasoning is based on false or faulty assumptions or feelings that we are not even aware of. We may deny or conveniently forget the facts we learn from others that do not support our own conclusions. Often, we can also misunderstand or distort what others say to fit into our own view.

Try to clear your mind, be present and aware of your own thoughts and feelings but be open to hearing other views. This is Inclusive Thinking.

POINT OF VIEW

As our perceptions come together, they help us to form our point of view (POV). We all have a POV that is uniquely our own. When we observe something or are given new information, how we interpret that information—what filters, lens and frames we use—are uniquely our own, and all contribute to how we make sense of what we see or hear, and what we think. This is how we create our own POV.

Being able to articulate your POV is important. However, what is most critical is to seek other people's POV, because it provides us—frequently—with a different way of seeing problems and solutions. This is a key component of Inclusive/Reflective thinking. If we only consider our own POV when observing and making decisions, we've left out the inclusive part of Inclusive/Reflective thinking. To be the most effective Essential Problem Solver, you need to use both Inclusive and Reflective thinking—Inclusive accepts others' points of view, which may include the best possible solutions to a problem, or even the best possible ways to define a problem, while Reflective thinking is used to take some time to wade through all the ideas generated, and to think about it, in order to determine which are best.

 Paul tries to be more open-minded himself, although he might not always show it. Terry, the new young manager for the Florida region, came in last month to ask if he could give the Miami store some free samples of a new Green Tea product. Paul's initial reaction was to say, "We don't do that around here anymore; we've gotten burned too often." Paul was remembering the last time he tried it when he invested a thousand dollars in chocolate that was distributed to local schools and Energize got nothing in return. When Paul saw the confused look on Terry's face, he immediately realized he wasn't listening to Terry's idea and was only coming from his own previous negative experience.

Paul decided to take some time to listen, reflect and take a fresh look at the current proposition Terry was presenting. After realizing that this was a very different situation from the one he had previously experienced, Paul was able to open his mind to hear and understand Terry's persuasive argument. Paul was then able to follow up on Terry's suggestion and ultimately give his idea a try.

It turned out to be a good lesson for both of them. Giving the Miami store free samples which they distributed to customers led to a big new Miami store order for Green Tea. It proved to Paul that being open-minded could lead to potential benefits and reinforced his belief that it was important to encourage this practice with his team.

STYLE PREFERENCES

Among the more crucial elements that affect our points of view are our style preferences. Most of us have preferences in the way we behave, think, and even manage people or conflicts. There are many varieties of assessments that have been created to measure and assess these preferences, including Myers-Briggs, DISC and NBI, which all have been used to explore style differences.

The Myers-Briggs Type Indicator is a self-reported questionnaire that identifies differing psychological preferences in how people perceive the world and make decisions. For instance, they might be asked if they prefer to focus more on the outer world or on their own inner world. This helps to identify if they are more of an Extrovert or an Introvert. Myers-Briggs identifies 16 different types of personalities. However, as they caution on their web site, "The goal of knowing about personality type is to understand and appreciate differences between people. As all types are equal, there is no best type."

The DISC assessment measures four different behavioral styles—Dominance, Influence, Steadiness and Conscientious—whereas NBI measures thinking style preferences—left brain versus right brain and concrete versus abstract. These assessments are widely used by many businesses and have proved very valuable in deepening an understanding of ourselves and others' styles, which help to make workplace interactions more effective, as well as more enjoyable.

Again, there are no best types or styles. The point is to know and understand your own innate style preferences, and to understand that another's style may differ from yours.

Paul consistently acknowledges and appreciates his and other employees' different style preferences through providing various types of recognition. When he implemented his Employee of the Month program, he made sure he used a variety of assessment tools and incentive possibilities.

He found out that Maria, a regional manager, liked to be rewarded privately, with him taking her to lunch at a fancy restaurant, whereas Diane liked to be recognized in public at the large monthly staff meeting. He knows these rewards have a significant effect on the employee's actions and thinking as well.

After Diane was honored last month, she immediately created a new recognition program for the store managers and their assistants in her region who had the highest monthly sales. An important aspect with any program, though, is to be sure you do it right and know your employees' reward preferences.

When pitching the program to upper management, he realized that the CEO, Mark, was a big picture thinker who liked to see how everything fit together. Paul made this assumption when Mark inquired, "How does the program fit into the company's vision?" Sam, the comptroller, on the other hand, seemed like an analytical/logical thinker, very concerned with the details and bottom line, as he questioned, "How will we pay for this down the road?"

Paul knew that neither perspective was right or wrong, only different, and it was essential to consider all points of view in creating an optimal program that addressed as many people's concerns and ideas as possible.

He proceeded to show Mark how the program would reinforce the company's focus on employee development and for Sam, that it could be funded as a part of each department's marketing budget.

Using this style preference information has helped Paul identify his and others' strengths and weaknesses to improve how they can best work together. He also found other style differences that provided keys to managing people.

Paul knows that Joyce, his North Carolina store manager, likes to work by herself and on one project at a time, while Tim and Roberto, two other store managers, find working in a team environment and on multiple projects more appealing, so he tries to accommodate them when he can. Sam, the company comptroller, has a preference for paying for everything in full, as projects move along. This aspect of his preferences certainly affects how open he and, in turn, the company can be to taking on risks.

Stay Curious!

Self-knowledge is the beginning of self-awareness. Learning our strengths and limitations can help us make the most of our interactions with other people and how we approach our job, as well as our approach to problems and solutions. Using assessment results about style preferences (Myers-Briggs, DISC, NBI) as guidelines for recognizing the similarities and differences between ourselves and the diverse people we work with can assist us in maximizing our communication and enhancing those relationships to make the most of our interactions.

CAUTION:

It's wise not to use the results of standardized assessments to label people and put them in a box.

Relying too much on these assessments limits our expectations of who they are and how they'll react. Everyone can react differently, depending upon the situation. Results of these assessments are simply indicators of certain tendencies in thinking and behavioral styles.

INCLUSIVE/REFLECTIVE THINKING

Inclusive/Reflective thinking is our ability to appreciate and comprehend the entire situation and deal effectively with all the different styles in issues we face. This helps us to find the best possible solutions and have the most effective responses. If we can broaden our insights, this will give us the ability to combine our thoughts and emotions with those of others we should take into consideration, i.e. those who are on our team, or working to define and solve a particular problem.

INCLUSIVE THINKING is having the awareness of our own thinking style preferences and limitations, combined with the ability to act using aspects of others' thinking styles.

REFLECTIVE THINKING is an active, persistent, and careful consideration of beliefs and the grounds that support and validate the knowledge that comes out of those beliefs. It is also the ability to remain open to further beliefs, conclusions and implications which that knowledge and other new information may lead us to.

Inclusive/Reflective Thinking focuses on showing us how we can use inclusion and reflection in our problem solving, and not respond with Automatic Thinking, which only uses the parts of our brain and ways of looking at situations with which we feel most comfortable.

Using Inclusive/Reflective thinking gives us a fuller and richer appreciation and understanding of the problems and challenges we encounter. This forms the basis of our Thinking It Through process, which will be discussed in more detail in later sections.

 Before Paul implemented his Employee of the Month program, he took some time to solicit ideas from a wide swath of employees to be sure he received the widest variety of possible ways to implement the program and offer incentive possibilities. Paul also took a few weeks after gathering the information to make some phone calls to be sure he was interpreting the data he collected correctly. This provided him the opportunity to reflect over everything he had, to see if there were any gaps. He also asked himself if he needed more information. And if he did, was it available? Who had the information? Would it be accurate? Could he find a way to get it? All of these were important questions to ask before he moved forward.

FEEDBACK

Getting feedback is a key mechanism in determining our blind spots—what people know about us and the situation we're dealing with that we don't know ourselves. Of course, our own openness to receiving others' feedback is vital. Defensiveness when receiving feedback can be a major roadblock to problem solving. It is only through our openness and respect for others' opinions that we can honestly see ourselves, the world, and problems and solutions as others see them.

Giving feedback is also a key to improving our relationships with those we work with and creating an open and honest communication environment for us to share our views and understand others' points of view.

The key word here is "communication," which is a two-way interaction. Before you can communicate effectively and clearly to an employee or team member to get the results you are looking for, you should listen to get an idea of that person's perspective, their POV, and their thinking styles.

 Paul realizes that another key to being a successful manager is to facilitate good communication. He does this by asking for feedback and giving feedback through both one-on-one and group meetings.

He also tries to serve as a role model by always providing open and honest feedback. This is an essential element that helps him and other employees understand how they're doing.

Paul had a bad experience recently where he hadn't told Ralph, one of his regional managers, that he had heard from Bob, the NC store manager, that he thought Ralph was being a bully. Bob told Paul that Ralph was constantly yelling at him and never listened to his perspective. Paul decided he would let the two of them work it out themselves. Bob suddenly quit and the company had a hard time replacing him.

Paul felt by not adequately doing the coaching part of his job and bringing them together, Ralph never got that feedback from Bob to understand his point of view. Paul believed this would have helped Ralph understand how Bob, and possibly others, viewed him.

It would certainly have helped Ralph learn and grow from hearing Bob's perspective. It might also have kept the company from losing Bob, a valued employee.

Paul now makes sure he goes well beyond annual performance review evaluations and sets up quarterly individual feedback meetings with everyone he supervises and requires his reps to do the same thing.

EMOTIONAL INTELLIGENCE (EQ)

Emotional Intelligence (EQ) is being knowledgeable about emotions and being able to respond to them effectively. EQ is the key to being able to recognize and positively manage emotions in oneself, in others, and in groups. It is impossible to be a successful problem solver without having good EQ.

The core elements involved in Emotional Intelligence are divided into two main areas:

PERSONAL COMPETENCE:

- **Self-Awareness** is knowing our internal emotional states—preferences, resources and intuitions—so that we can manage ourselves competently.

- **Self- Management** is how we see and manage our own emotions and ourselves.

SOCIAL COMPETENCE:

- **Social Awareness** is an awareness of others' emotions, feelings, needs and concerns.

- **Relationship Management** is your ability to build your interpersonal effectiveness. Strengthening bonds with others through effective communication to help generate and sustain trust is central to relationship-building and management.

Paul knows he needs to be aware of how he and others recognize and respond to their own and others' emotions and styles. He realizes he must be able to assess his own ability to understand, tolerate and interact with others in emotional situations.

Only then can he help the people he supervises do the same for the people they supervise.

At a recent staff meeting two of Paul's managers made that point quite clearly when Maria sat with her arms crossed and a scowl on her face, as Ralph loudly seemed to criticize her in front of everyone for not informing him about a customer complaint regarding the South Carolina store he supported.

Paul had to pull Ralph to the side to have a private conversation with him to be sure that Ralph knew this was a situation that could have been handled much better off-line and in a private one-on-one conversation with Maria.

REAL LIFE EXAMPLES

Think of a problem you're facing on your job right now, or one which you faced recently. It could be about working with customers, implementing a new product, integrating a new process, or any situation in which you were faced with a problem. It should be a real problem and possibly one that affected others on your team as well as yourself. How did your awareness of yourself, those involved, and the circumstances surrounding the situation affect your perspective?

- How does awareness of self and others' perceptions play a role in your view of this problem?

- What's your point of view about the problem? How did you arrive at this point of view?

- How might your style preferences affect the way you view the problem and possible solutions?

- What part did your emotions play in this situation?

- What kind of feedback have you already gotten from others about your perception of the problem?

Step 2.
Define the Problem

Being sure we define the right problem is one of the most important elements of the process. We need to be sure we're not just dealing with a symptom and that we have identified the essential problem. This is the point where we need to stop and think, in order to start at a place where we can get beyond our Automatic Thinking view of the situation. We must take into our awareness various aspects of the problem to get an all-encompassing perspective. It may take a considerable amount of time to accurately articulate the problem, but it's crucial to the success of this problem-solving method.

Ultimately, we need to express the problem as an open-ended question to jump start our thinking, for example:

Open-ended Question: What types of things may have led to the decline in sales last quarter? (The question encourages an exploration of the problem and its symptoms and input from more than just one person.)

Closed-ended Question: Is the decline in sales due to our need for more salespeople? (The answer can only be "yes" or "no" or even "maybe," but the question invites only a one-word answer.)

USING AUTOMATIC THINKING

Sometimes when we're faced with solving a problem, there are constraints such as time and budgets which leave us no choice but to define and solve the problem in a short period of time and possibly by ourselves. There is little time to think. We must simply act. We refer to this process of solving problems as Automatic Thinking. However, in the workplace, we are more frequently tasked with working with other people to explore problems and devise solutions. We refer to this process as Inclusive/Reflective Thinking.

In a situation in which a manager or employee has no choice but to solve problems on their own, many times they assume they already know what the problem is and the solution to it, and so they proceed automatically to solve the problem on their own. Perhaps they have past experience with similar problems, and therefore think the same solution will solve a similar problem. Or maybe they feel that if they are in charge of the situation or responsible for a particular area, they should therefore somehow already know how to solve the problem on their own. Unfortunately, problem solving based on personal assumptions like these don't always lead to good solutions.

What you expect is usually what you get.

What are you expecting?

We frequently use Automatic Thinking—making statements or assumptions without having thought them through. We receive information, automatically feel we recognize what it means, and then automatically respond in the way we believe is appropriate.

One of Paul's regional managers, Diane, who has oversight of the store in Atlanta, was responsible for assessing why the store was losing money and employees. While currently fully staffed, it was having a lot of employee turnover and also running in the red over the last six months.

At the recent regional managers meeting where this problem was discussed, Ralph thought he knew exactly what the problem was, because he'd "seen it before" in the South Carolina store—the manager was just not hiring the "right" people.

Based on that assumption, Ralph felt strongly and suggested that Diane immediately read the riot act to Tim, the Atlanta store manager, "to order him to get rid of the dead wood and hire people with the right skills and attitude, period, the end."

However, Diane thought the problem was that the new hires were not getting enough direction and training. When Diane had visited the store the previous month, she noticed a number of people were either wasting time talking to each other in the stock room or doing less important things like picking up trash or stacking shelves. Meanwhile, people were desperately needed up front, as long lines were forming at the cash registers and staff wasn't responding.

On the other hand, Maria, another regional manager, whose store in D.C. recently went through what she thought was a similar experience to Atlanta's, felt they just needed to hire more staff, as the D.C. store did, to be successful in fixing their similar problem.

Paul realized how many times he's looked at situations and compared them with ones he'd already experienced. All too often, he's given the information from those past experiences more weight in his assessment of current situations without taking into consideration the uniqueness of this new situation. He remembers that using Automatic Thinking and response on many occasions has led him to think he recognized a problem, knew the solution and then acted on it. It's not that taking these past experiences into consideration wasn't helpful, but he had learned that it might play too much of a part in an instant analysis and response to the current problem.

HOW WE PROCESS INFORMATION THROUGH
AUTOMATIC THINKING

Receive: We take in information—receive it through our senses, our eyes and ears, as well as our senses of touch and taste and smell. It's estimated that we are exposed to millions of pieces of information coming at us through our senses every second, ten million through our eyes alone. Our mind selects a specific number of these to focus on.

Recognize: We recognize the situation based on comparisons to something we already know or have experienced before. As the new information passes through our personal filters/lenses/frames and feelings, we evaluate the incoming sensory information we've received and automatically come to a prediction about what it means.

Since many of our expectations are based on past knowledge and experience, this sometimes predisposes us to focus on specific areas and/or assign specific meanings and make assumptions. Assumption-making sometimes works in conjunction with one or more of these types of perceptions:

Pattern Recognition: This is another way of describing how our thinking works to fit this new information we've received into what we already know. Our minds sometimes actually have to fill in the gaps and bend the information to fit it into what we already know. This happens especially when we can't easily categorize something—it's unknown or ambiguous—and we have to respond to not knowing by coming up with an explanation that fits into a recognizable pattern.

Projection: When there is a gap in our knowledge—when new information doesn't fit into a predictable pattern—

we sometimes project our thoughts or feelings in order to have a "logical" explanation. For instance, if you thought someone hid important information in the past, you may think they are not being totally honest with you in the current situation.

This is sometimes accompanied by the "you get what you expect" syndrome, or the "self-fulfilling prophecy," where events turn out as you hypothesized. This expected outcome is not a result of a great insight on your part, but a result of having focused on only some specific information that supports your prior beliefs. However, ignoring information that does not support your projected belief or conclusion can cause an inaccurate guess.

Respond:
We then respond to the problem—sometimes by taking no action—based on our assumptions and expectations about this particular type of problem and how it should be solved.

This helps set up a reflective loop process that feeds back into our beliefs, which we then take in as "fact." We use those "facts" as knowledge again the next time we encounter a similar problem, which reinforces our subsequent assumptions, conclusions, beliefs, expectations and/or actions—even though these new facts may not completely support our previous assumptions.

Although Automatic Thinking is an important system that helps us live our lives more efficiently, it can also deceive us into prematurely defining our views, and influence us into making decisions and responding to certain situations in a pre-determined, automatic way.

It's incredible to realize how much of the time we engage in Automatic Thinking, making assumptions, drawing conclusions, having inferences from them and acting on what we then believe to be true—only to realize later that the solutions we thought were perfect for that particular problem did not work out.

To re-cap, using Paul's situation described above as an example:

Receive—Sensory information (what you see, hear, smell, taste, feel) points to the problem.
Problem: I can see from the sales reports that our store is losing money.

Recognize—Knowledge, past experiences, values, patterns are used to make assumptions when identifying the problem.
Identify the Problem: The store's loss of money is due to:
- Not hiring the right people (Ralph)
- Employees not getting the right training and direction (Diane)
- The need to hire more employees (Maria)

Respond—Take action, or not, based on how the problem was recognized and identified.
Solution:
- Fire the wrong people and hire the right people (Ralph)
- Get more training and direction for the employees (Diane)
- Hire more employees (Maria)

USING INCLUSIVE/REFLECTIVE THINKING

This is the most important time, when we pause before we move from the Recognize stage to the Respond stage—the Stop & Think moment. This moment, and the options it provides, is a focal point of this book and one of the keys to becoming an Essential Problem Solver.

As we've seen, Automatic Thinking is sometimes inevitable, due to the constraints of time and ease of use, but it's a path that can be laden with obstacles, if the goal is to find the best solutions to problems.

When we're basically going it alone, relying only on our own instant interpretations of a problem and how to solve it—using only our own limited filters, frames, lenses, points of view, experiences and established patterns without questioning them—the solution to the problem may be doomed from the start.

What we need to do is examine the similarities with the former experiences we're looking at, but also explore the differences. Since no two situations are exactly the same, this will give us the chance to explore the uniqueness of our current problem.

Using Inclusive and Reflective Thinking gives us the opportunity to review our facts and data, take the time to collect, clarify and confirm the information, and also to include additional data and consider other points of view in order to decipher what it all means. In short, when we are more inclusive in how we gather information and feedback about perceived problems, we will be able to work towards better solutions, especially when we also include the process of reflection. This addition of using the process of Inclusive and Reflective Thinking helps us to integrate both logic and emotion.

FILTERS/LENSES/FRAMES

Filters—also known as lenses or frames—play an important part in all our thinking. Imagine that, as the old saying goes, you look at the world through rose-colored glasses or lenses. Or think about what you'd see if when you took a photograph of a tree with a close-up frame so that you only saw the bark and not the leaves. In this same way, we apply filters, lenses, and frames to how we view problems.

Filters, lenses and frames provide the connection between taking in sensory data and the assumptions we make. Given the amount of information our minds process daily, our approach to making meaning of it all rests strongly upon our need to quickly recognize, identify, and make assumptions about this new information.

As we interpret the various sensory data that comes into our focus, the only thing that we can be sure of is that no two of us will interpret that information exactly the same way and come up with identical assumptions and conclusions. Each of our own individual filters/lenses/frames are unique, and so subsequent predictions based on the exact same data will be different among diverse people.

There are many elements that shape our individual filters, including our family backgrounds, education, life experiences, feelings and values. More importantly, our interpretation of our life events and information is unique. With time, mental models begin to form and specific set ways of interpreting new information and experiences become ingrained in each of us, and we develop unquestioned habits about how to sift through the information, understand it and react in the world.

These filters/lenses/frames we are seeing through also have to do with context—who and where we are. Our context plays into how we frame any issue or situation. For example, if we are the controller of a company, we may look at something through a financial lens, but if we are in human resources, we may be seeing something from a people lens, or even a compliance lens.

Paul knows that how we were brought up, the experiences that we've had in life, and our interpretations and feelings about them, help create filters through which we assess new situations. For that reason, he knows that over time we build up mental models and strong expectations of how things should be. Paul understands this can lead to big problems when people, including himself, use Automatic Thinking to interpret and respond to problems that may arise.

When he worked for a supermarket chain, before coming to Energize Foods, Paul was having some problems with the union. He presumed that they would always protect their members under any circumstances. Upon encountering a union member being accused of the serious complaint of stealing products, he thought that the union rep would protect this member at all costs. So, when Paul met with the union rep, he started out with a combative attitude.

Paul's reactive thinking would probably be the same as the immediate reaction of many managers whose mental models were forged solely by their previous bad experiences with union reps on union complaints. Managers who have had good or no experiences working with union reps would, of course, have a different reaction, because they would not have yet formed any preconceived patterns about having to work with union reps.

Fortunately, Paul was able to recognize his automatic belief was not always correct, and after that, he was able to approach similar situations with a more unbiased view, enabling him to work things out with the impartial union representative.

A mental model is

"The image of the world around us,

which we carry in our head."

—Jay Wright Forrester

VALUES AND BELIEFS

Our values and beliefs play an important role in our filters. They affect the way we think as much as logic does, and they help form the bedrock of our thinking. Our values and beliefs are the basis of our filtering system and aid in shaping our mental models and set ways of thinking, the frameworks that inform our perceptions. They are also at the core of our automatic thinking process.

Beliefs set up specific ways of thinking or feeling and sometimes become mental models that we use to interpret the world. Automatic believing occurs when we intuitively believe everything we see and hear without questioning it, when "seeing is believing." We rapidly—automatically—assess whether what we're seeing or sensing, and how we're interpreting it, is true or not. Then we consequently reject it if it doesn't fit into what we believe is true, or continue to believe these things if they line up with our beliefs.

When what we see is based on what we believe, this helps us form our models of reality. This can be especially problematic when we misinterpret people and events.

Truth is subjective and depends largely on our past experience and current knowledge. Subsequently, truth depends on the belief systems that we've created as a result of those experiences and the knowledge we've generated from them.

> ## "We don't see things as they are, we see things as we are."
>
> — Anais Nin

MENTAL MODELS

Mental models are the sets of firm ideas, beliefs and feelings that we alluded to in the previous section, that often guide our actions.

We frequently use them to explain "cause and effect" situations and to give meaning to our experiences. Our mental models help shape our behavior and define our approach to solving problems and carrying out tasks.

ADAPTIVE UNCONSCIOUS AND CONSCIOUSNESS

The last element we'll look at in this section is how we sometimes consciously and other times unconsciously assess our world. As we've discussed, a good deal of human perception, memory and action is unconscious and automatic. This method serves as an internal pattern detector which helps us by automatically selecting, interpreting and evaluating data.

When we are using Automatic Thinking and working in the Adaptive Unconscious mode, how can we attain accurate self-insight? It is certainly not done best through introspection, since it is hard for us to take a truly objective look at ourselves.

Sometimes we see in others' behaviors or in what's happening around us exactly what we are expecting to see, even when it might not be there. In these cases, we frequently get exactly what we expect. So, it is extremely important to examine our anticipated thoughts and feelings and expectations and not let them dictate our conclusions and responses. For instance, Paul's expectations about union reps led him to believe he was in for a fight when he sought to address an employee problem. The reality was completely different, when he discovered that the union rep handled the situation sympathetically and with an open mind.

It is only natural that we sometimes unconsciously assess the world around us and new information coming in. As we've discussed, a good deal of human perception, memory and action is unconscious and automatic.

Automatic Thinking helps us by automatically selecting, interpreting and evaluating data based on what we already know or have experienced. If we are using Automatic Thinking, we are working in the Adaptive Unconscious mode. This might be helpful or useful in a situation which calls for instant action. However, most situations in life, especially in the workplace, demand that we Stop & Think before drawing conclusions and jumping into action.

We are constantly bombarded with events, messages, and other information that we absorb through our five senses each and every day. So, it is crucial that we are able to accurately decode this information to clearly make sense of our world, especially in the workplace.

 Paul remembers his experience last year driving along Route 101 in Georgia. He'd been on that highway many times before, since he visits the Atlanta store at least three times a year. Suddenly Paul realized that he'd been on automatic pilot for miles, unaware of the road or other vehicles. He was preoccupied, thinking about the upcoming meeting with Tim, the store manager, where he was planning to present his ideas about a current business challenge.

It was scary for Paul to realize that for the past half hour he was not consciously aware of anything around him. The routine of the drive kept him from being present and mindful and kept his consciousness tuned out to what was happening on the road. Paul then understood that this explained his need to jam on the brakes when he hadn't even noticed a car on his left moving into his lane.

In another situation, Paul had to attend a meeting with an important supplier because Pam, the South Carolina store manager, could not attend. Pam told Paul that this particular supplier was argumentative and always asked self-serving stupid questions.

After the meeting with the supplier and others, Paul commiserated with Pam when they met. He pointed out how right she was and agreed with her about how argumentative John, the supplier, was. Paul then started to recite all the self-serving, stupid questions John asked.

The only problem was that when Paul mentioned the supplier's name—John—it turned out that it was not John that Pam was talking about, it was Charley.

Another example played out at a recent meeting when Mark, the company president, asked for ideas about reorganizing the company.

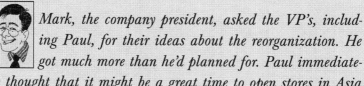

Mark, the company president, asked the VP's, including Paul, for their ideas about the reorganization. He got much more than he'd planned for. Paul immediately thought that it might be a great time to open stores in Asia and Mexico, as some of their competitors had done. Bill, the VP of marketing, came in with a report focusing on an idea that

he'd had for a while, on how the company could expand their product offerings to appeal to more diverse customers. Donna, the VP of Procurements, had some serious reservations, and quickly came up with a list of questions and concerns she had about how the move might cause confusion and disruption among suppliers.

Only Elizabeth, the VP of Sales, seemed to understand what Mark was asking. She came in with a well thought out and balanced look at where the company was and where it might go in the future. She gave a broad overview and a detailed plan of how Energize might take a step-by-step approach to increasing their presence in current areas where they were doing well.

She had taken the time to collect all the necessary information, clarify the data and draw a few thoughtful conclusions, as well as consider some possible consequences. Finally, she suggested how Energize might slowly expand in a measured way into new markets. Her presentation included many different perspectives and was very thoughtfully delivered.

What Mark was looking for was exactly what Elizabeth prepared, a broad-brush look at where the company was and some general well-thought-out ideas of where it might go next. Unfortunately, Paul and others responded automatically only from their own perspectives and interpretations of Mark's question.

It is mainly through consciously looking at our behavior and how others react to it that helps us become more aware of who we are and how we make decisions. Investigating what we do and assessing others' reactions to that can positively affect the way we look at our lives and how we are seen in the world, and how we operate in the workplace.

It is from this perspective that we can truly get an outsider's objective view and make the best possible decisions about what alterations need to be made.

In the next Section, we'll explore how we can modify our overuse of Automatic Thinking and engage in more Inclusive/ Reflective thinking, which is what we'll need to become an Essential Problem Solver.

REAL LIFE EXAMPLES

Think back to your own workplace problem that you defined in the previous chapter or think of a new one that you've recently faced. Try to state it as an open-ended question—one that can't be answered with just a "yes" or "no" or a one-word answer. If you can do that, you'll have a head start in thinking about possible solutions.

- Is your definition of the problem clear and specific, and does it deal with the heart of the issue?

- What ways has Automatic Thinking played a part in your view of the problem?

- What makes up your filters and what part do they play in how you see your situation?

- How have your "mental models" affected your assessment of the situation?

- Have you considered other ways of looking at and stating your problem definition?

Step 3
Explore the Problem

The Thinking It Through process should be implemented after you take the opportunity to stop and think and use the time to step back and see if there's anything in the here and now or immediate future that might be affecting the way you are—or should be—looking at your assessment of the situation.

There could be a time crunch, political or additional factors influencing your evaluation, or other unique components that might be affecting your interpretation of the problem. It might also be important at this point to take a moment to explore whether you or others involved have anything on a specific or broader level—either personally or environmentally—that might affect your views.

It is at this point that you might decide to further explore assessing your beliefs and feelings about the problem. How can you take a more critical look at the information you've gathered and the processes you're using to come to your conclusions and beliefs, but before making your response to the problem?

"If I had an hour to solve a problem, I'd take the first 55 minutes understanding the problem, and the last 5 minutes solving it."

—Albert Einstein

To maximize the quality of our thinking, we must learn how to become effective critics of our own thinking. Exploring our values, biases and the way we are framing issues and situations has much to do with how we perceive them. Using reflection, listening, asking questions and investigation will give us our best assessment of an issue, situation or challenge, as we move on to the next steps. During this process of Inclusive/Reflective thinking, we will also examine our feelings and others' feelings as well, as they relate to the problem at hand.

Ask yourself and others some basic questions:
What do we believe is true?
How do we know it to be true?
Could it be anything else?

THE THINKING IT THROUGH PROCESS — USING INCLUSIVE/REFLECTIVE THINKING

The process presented below, the Thinking It Through Process, gives us a specific way to explore more deeply the problems, issues or challenges we face.

Collect—Assess Information
- What data are you using to support or clarify your beliefs? Is it verifiable?
- What other information will you need to know? Is it available? Will it be credible?

Clarify—Recognize Assumptions & Analyze Evidence
- What beliefs, attitudes, feelings/ideas are you working with?
- What is your evidence and how solid is it? Are there other assumptions you can make?

Confirm—Explore Conclusions, Consequences & Implications

- What conclusions can you reach as a result of those assumptions and evidence?

- What investigation or reasoning have you used in drawing these conclusions?

- What, if any, are the possible implications or consequences as a result of these conclusions?

Consider—Other Points of View

- From what point of view are you considering this issue?

- What other perspectives should you be considering?

To go back to an earlier situation, Paul had asked Diane, a regional manager, to work with Tim, the Atlanta store manager, to collect all the pertinent data and information to assess why that store, though it was now fully staffed, was still having a lot of employee turnover and also running in the red over the last six months.

Diane realized that, although she should take her experiences and others' past experiences into consideration, it was most important to see what was different in this current situation. She remembered that what you perceive is not a simple black-and-white process of being either this or that. Diane realized there might be many elements that were similar, but others that might be quite unique. It seemed similar to a situation two years earlier, when her North Carolina store was losing customers, so Diane immediately looked for problems within the store. However, instead of just reacting to her initial perception of the problem, which was that the store didn't have enough adequately trained staff as in North Carolina, she decided to take some time to seriously look into all the aspects that might be currently affecting this situation.

After some preliminary investigation in which she canvassed the employees and customers, Diane realized that the smaller number of customers might more importantly have to do with the expansion and recent increase in publicity for a new grocery chain in an adjacent community and not necessarily a lower interest in coming to the Energize store.

This was an important fact for Diane to keep in mind during her next phone call with Tim. She needed to discuss what kind of information they would need to collect and how they would obtain it. Tim suggested he already knew what the problem was in Atlanta, and also the solution. "It's simple," he said, "The most important issue is store profitability and to achieve that, we have to raise some prices and cut a few employee benefits—maybe like raising the employee share of the skyrocketing medical insurance costs." Tim also thought that they needed to act quickly and that collecting "a whole bunch of extraneous information," as he put it, "would be a big waste of time."

Diane didn't say much yet, but she thought it wasn't as clear cut as Tim surmised. She especially felt that raising the insurance costs for employees might only add to the current turnover problem. Diane and Tim decided during their next phone call to take a few days to think it over, do some research and come up with some specific ideas and options. They would then set up an in-person meeting in the next few weeks to make some decisions and decide on what other information they might need to move forward.

1. COLLECT

Get the facts/information/feelings to be sure you've gathered all relevant data.

"You must thoroughly diagnose before you can accurately prescribe."

—Stephen Covey

We need to take the time to be present, mindful and able to clearly see what information is available. In our effort to collect all relevant data, facts and feelings, we also need to be aware of the role diversity plays. The kinds of information we're exposed to and our ability to collect all the data we need is important—most likely we'll have to research what additional data we'll need, and who will provide it. Also, deciding how we will interpret that data, is a crucial element for collecting. For instance, if we decide we need to survey customers, what questions will we ask? It's important to think about it because the answers we get will depend upon the questions we ask.

Taking the tact of slow knowing and allowing time to take in and process the data is essential. Trying to be comfortable with ambiguity, and not knowing, will also help us to better understand the issue or situation. Investigating those areas of uncertainty will help us know what we know, what we don't know, and what we need to know.

Listening and observing are key components of Inclusive Thinking in this stage of Collecting information. We not only need to really listen to what is being said, but what is also not being said. Silence, sometimes known as "the elephant in the room," is what people either don't want to talk about or don't even think to discuss. Silence is also a matter of nonverbal clues, or what is being said through body language. Remember—everyone needs to be heard and understood, but they may not be able to communicate explicitly with only their words.

In order to develop that objective awareness and ability to listen, we need to take into account two important factors as we go about collecting information to define and resolve the problem:

Content: words/tone, body language, feelings, and even silence—what's NOT being said—from others who are affected by the problem and/or invested in resolving it.

Context: what's on-going in the general and specific environment you're operating in, i.e. the importance placed on the problem, the urgency of the problem, timing and deadlines for resolving the problem, distractions from the problem. Others' input, intuition, and experiences, as well as the resources available, will be critical elements to consider.

As Diane thought about the Atlanta situation, she felt it would be essential to first get others' input and find out their points of view. After having a meeting with Paul, Bill, the Marketing Manager, and a number of her peers, Diane came up with a good list of the types of information that would help her and Tim to accurately assess the situation. An important element was being mindful and taking the time to get both employee and customer feedback.

When Diane sent Tim the question list prior to their meeting, he called her and was annoyed, angry and dismissive. "This is a complete waste of time!" he shouted into the phone. "Why do you think it's a waste of time?" Diane inquired. "Why do we need to ask all these questions?" he complained. "I know what we should do to fix this, because I've experienced this kind of situation many times before in my career," Tim continued, "and the more time we wait the worse it will get."

Diane decided to meet with Paul again before she met with Tim. After hearing Diane's logic, Paul said he, too, thought it was a good idea to collect an adequate amount of information before taking action. "We want to be sure we get this right," Paul said. "Unless we take the time to look at this as the unique situation it is, we might make the mistake of seeing it as something else we've experienced before and not really understand this specific situation. Diane, you've got great people skills, so I trust that you'll be able to handle this when you meet with Tim," Paul assured her, "but if you ultimately need backup, I'll be there to help."

Mindfulness means "being present" and is another essential element of the collecting process. It is by being present in the here and now that we are able to accurately see what is going on right here, right now, and not be distracted by what's gone on in the past or what we think might happen in the future. This is an important element of our being able to accurately observe any issue, situation or challenge in its current state.

 On the plane to Atlanta, Diane felt much better knowing she had Paul's support. While flying, she took some time to go over her notes and some of the questions she felt

should be on the customer surveys. It was also important how they should word them, so the customers could truly understand what was being asked, especially if English wasn't their first language. She soon realized that the cultural backgrounds of the customers and employees might play an important part in what and how each person saw the situation at the store and the answers they'd provide. Diane thought that she and Tim might have to have a number of person-to-person meetings, because just filling out surveys might not be the best way to gather the most accurate information.

This was especially important since they had a large Hispanic and Asian customer population who might be better able to get their point across through face-to-face conversations. She knew from her past experience with the North Carolina store that when seeking good feedback, these populations might not be as comfortable filling out surveys.

Diane also remembered that at the Miami store with face-to-face meetings, she and Roberto, the store manager, could observe nonverbals—customers' body language—and also what the customers didn't say, which was sometimes even more important than what they did say. For the employees, they might be less likely to write down what they really think and feel because of possible management repercussions, so Diane knew nonverbals would be critical there too.

Diversity/Cultural: Diversity comes in many forms and is an important factor in some of the critical aspects of collecting data in the workplace. Do we view particular information as significant or not? Who is the information coming from? Have we included everyone who should be included when gathering the information we need? Have we taken into account elements like conversational style and even relationships between those who are gathering the information and those who are providing it?

How we take in that data, from big picture to detailed, will affect our focus and can ultimately shape our interpretation. Taking into account the various backgrounds and experiences of the responders and collectors will also be central in gathering data.

 It turned out that Diane's meeting with Tim went better than expected, as she felt they were able to hear and understand each other's point of view. Diane was focusing on the overall long-term success of the Atlanta store, while Tim's major concern was the store's profitability, especially since his bonus depended on it.

Diane still had a hard time convincing Tim that they needed to find out not only what others—i.e., employees and customers—thought, but how they felt. Tim eventually came around to understand that asking questions would really help them be aware of the problem from many other points of view. After the meeting, Diane created a list of questions that she and Tim would use covering three areas:

Employees: *What is the state of the staffing? How many PT and FT employees do we currently have? How many people have left and why? Have there been any work pattern changes? i.e. more overtime required or a change in work schedules? Have there been any major personnel changes before or since these issues had begun? What did the employees think might help retain employees?*

Customers: *How have the numbers of customers and times they have been shopping changed? Have any of them complained or asked questions? Have we asked for their suggestions?*

The Store: *Is there anything else that has occurred in the store or any outside factors that might have affected the current situation? What effects, if any, have these issues had on staff, customers, vendors, etc.? What has Tim tried already to fix any of these issues?*

Diane and Tim also decided that after they collected the entire customer and employee survey information, they would also be sure to state their own thoughts and feelings about what the problems and solutions were as well as how they might decide on next steps.

Exploring the information gathered, both the quantity and quality, will help us determine whether we'll need to look further. We need to be sure we have all the adequate data and a clear system to assess what everything means and how it fits together. Some questions we might ask at this stage would be:

- Have we been selective with the information we've been exposed to?

- Are there any elements of the information we're interpreting that are not lining up? For instance, when the words, tone and body language of the customers aren't saying the same thing?

- Do we need additional data?

- Is additional data or information available? If so, would it be verifiable?

- What would it mean if we don't get any additional data or information?

After Diane and Tim collected all the customer and employee survey information, they also conducted individual customer and employee interviews with the assistance of a few of the department managers.

This helped identify which information they collected by survey could be substantiated, negated or enhanced by in-person responses.

Diane knew she had to take into consideration Tim's feeling of being under pressure and that the home office was intent on getting the Atlanta store's challenges under control as soon as possible. That's why she understood Tim's impatience with getting to work on the issues. She also knew they had to take time to deliberate and think over the information they had gathered to come up with a successful resolution.

Slow Knowing means taking the time to not only collect all the data but to assess your thoughts and feelings about that information as you go about the collection process. This is critical in the collecting phase and involves Reflective Thinking. It is through reflection, exploring uncertainty, and questioning your findings, that new and useful information can be unearthed and discerned. Sometimes it can also be important to spend time exploring your questions to see if by making adjustments, it may even lead to better questions.

"The man who knows he doesn't know is the wisest of all."
- Socrates

Diane and Tim recognized that they might also have to take some time and be comfortable with not immediately knowing exactly what the problem is, as well as what the answers might be in needing to solve the Atlanta store's problems. Contemplating what came out of the information helped them to fully understand all the data they gathered before coming up with the possible solutions. However, it was also helpful that they were able to take some time to be comfortable "not knowing" exactly what something was. This allowed them to arrive at their best answers.

By fully using the process of reflective thinking, Diane and Tim were able to think long and hard about their findings. They were also able to take into consideration how others felt about the issues, as well as what their own instincts told them.

This was a critical action, or in this case an inaction, that Diane and Tim took when they decided to wait before moving to the important next steps of clarifying and confirming.

Ambiguity: Good managers and decision-makers learn to become comfortable with not always knowing exactly what something means, or not knowing it right away.

In Diane and Tim's case, they knew that they knew some of the answers, but they weren't sure yet what some of the information they'd collected meant. By deciding to wait before jumping to conclusions, it gave them time to pay more attention to the data and information they had already collected, and also to figure out if they needed more information, or time to sift through what they had in order to make sense of it.

Understanding that if we take our time to notice the particulars of a certain situation, issue or challenge, we will be able to pick up subtle nuances we may have missed at first. With a little time, things that are ambiguous at first can be seen in a much clearer way.

2. CLARIFY

Clarifying is the point at which we need to ask questions about the information we've gathered so far, including examining our assumptions, and deciding how to do further in-depth analysis.

 After thinking about the information they had gathered, Diane and Tim recruited two Atlanta store department managers to help collect the surveys. They enlisted them to help follow up and complete the interviews they needed in order to move to the next step of clarifying the information. The questions they asked themselves at this point were: What information should we focus on? How do we verify its credibility? In looking through the survey and interview data collected, Diane and Tim had to take some time to fully understand the feedback they received. The different types of people they solicited information from had their own assumptions and beliefs about the store and what was true:

Customers: *said they wanted more information on, and greater availability to, products, both less expensive alternatives and additional higher end products. They also wanted the store to be open at different hours.*

Employees: *wanted extra flexibility, i.e. students wanted to be able to shift their hours to accommodate their school schedules, while others wanted opportunities to make more money through* *working overtime or being given more challenging responsibilities. One said he was performing tasks that were "a waste of my time."*

The Store: *Tim's one overriding concern was to have the store be profitable and to a lesser degree, decrease staff turnover.*

An important new element Diane and Tim learned as they collected information was that a new competing store that had opened in an adjacent neighborhood was offering some similar products and an expanded array of products, and that on some days, they were open earlier and closed later. How much influence this new store's opening was having on the Energize store's situation was still something Diane and Tim had to explore. Through the personal interviews, Diane and Tim were also able to see if the words, tone and body language matched, when people spoke about their thoughts and feelings concerning the store.

How Diane and Tim went about examining all these assumptions was crucial in clarifying the information they had collected. As an example, when one of the customers was asked by Diane whether she felt the products Energize provided were adequate, although the answer was yes, the customer usually looked away when responding to the interviewer and her tone of voice didn't seem to conform to what she had said. Diane remembered that this happened in her experience with the North Carolina store when some of the customers didn't want to appear to be disrespectful because they might be seen as criticizing the store. However, rather than just assuming that the same thing was happening in this interview, Diane ran her interpretation by Tim.

Diane and Tim took the information from employees and customers they had collected and analyzed it by creating a chart of the problem areas they had identified:

> **Customers:** *want more information and greater product availability; expanded hours for store.*
>
> **Employees:** *want opportunities to make more money and more flexibility in their working hours.*
>
> **Store:** *has been unprofitable for the last six months, and a competing store has recently expanded their hours and seems to be offering more product selections.*

Assumptions/Beliefs

This is where we explore what we assume and believe is true, in order to determine if it is, indeed, true. Assessing where these beliefs come from and what the evidence, or lack of evidence, is for our assumptions is instrumental in the clarification process. Many times, our feelings play an important part in what we believe is true.

By asking great questions, we will be able to collect all the information that's needed, and then clarify its validity. Yet another key component for collecting and clarifying information is to really listen to what is being said with words, and what is not being said, but perhaps suggested through nonverbals.

Biases/Attributions

You can make assumptions, but you need to beware of biases. As we have discussed, in the process of making assumptions, we are very likely to become a victim of our own biases, values, and our preconceived notions of what we believe to be true or "real."

To begin to clarify our beliefs and the information collected, we need to be aware of the biases and prejudices we're bringing with us, which might be affecting our outlook.

Also, how and why we're making our attributions is significant. Thinking that we already know the reasons behind what people are thinking, doing, or not doing can lead to erroneous conclusions.

Some common biases are:

Overconfidence bias: placing too much faith in your knowledge, opinions and judgements.

Confirmation bias: searching for and recalling only the information which supports your prior beliefs.

Groupthink is also important to take into consideration. Groupthink is when there's a powerful desire for conformity regardless of one's own personal beliefs. Many times, this stops people from stating their own thoughts and ideas, or from really having them heard, even when they do want to express them. For these reasons unfortunately, groupthink can frequently result in irrational or bad decision-making.

Reflecting on the information we've gathered or received by being well aware of our own mindsets is a critically important element in the process. By asking great questions and doing investigation, we can many times get the information that's needed to define and solve a problem. However, we need to use Reflective Thinking at this point—taking the time to stop and reflect on the data we've collected, our own biases, and the mindset of the people who are giving us that information.

An initial concern Diane and Tim needed to deal with as they started their analysis of the Atlanta store, was to look at what biases and prejudices they were bringing to the situation. Diane knew that she was biased by her recent experience with the North Carolina store, which affected how she was viewing this Atlanta store situation. She also thought she was possibly giving more weight to that past event than it deserved.

Diane learned in discussions with Tim that a lot of his resistance to taking the time to collect the data came from his experience at a former job. His boss wanted to take time to survey customers before introducing a new product. By the time they collected and analyzed the results, they missed the market and a competitor got way ahead of them and captured most of the profits by getting the product out first.

After their discussions, both Diane and Tim knew they had to thoughtfully assess the experiences they've had, to see how relevant those biases might be in this current situation. They knew they needed to carefully look at how much they were attributing the problem to just internal Energize store issues. They thought they should also explore the role the new store in the area might be playing with these issues.

Values are powerful drivers of how we think, feel and behave. Our values are formed by what we've learned and experienced in our lives, as well as the societal norms we conform to. Understanding the part our values play in interpreting how we are viewing the world is a key component in clarifying the information we gather as we work towards defining a problem and finding solutions.

How we define specific values and interpret their importance is very critical in reaching an understanding with others.

Two issues that Diane and Tim agreed on very strongly were that they highly valued getting honest input from both customers and employees. They also agreed that the company values of always offering "the best products at the lowest prices" would be paramount in their deliberations.

On the other hand, they knew they might have to consider operating outside of these basic company values in looking at adding new higher end or other types of products, if that was what the customers really wanted.

Framing/Reframing is about the way we position what we're seeing. This affects not only our initial view of a problem, but also how we explore the situation. Looking at an issue in a negative light, we may tend to look for information that just reinforces that belief. An example would be a company comptroller might view a new acquisition from a primarily financial perspective and if the company is currently having money problems, would pay less attention to other positive aspects of the situation.

Anchoring is drawing on an initial or specific piece of information which we then use to compare against other incoming data. In a negotiation, for example, we may anchor on the first initial bid from the other party and this might unconsciously have an over-emphasized effect on the bid we make. So, if the other party bid $2,000, our bid will be somewhere around the $2,000 level also—even though realistically, the facts tell us we should have bid higher in order to cover costs and have an adequate margin.

Before Diane and Tim dove into an in-depth investigation of the issues, they wanted to be sure they were looking at the situation through a similar frame of reference. Should they be considering the profit problem as the most crucial frame to use and consider only how their Energize store could stop losing money? And with staff, how could they reduce employee turnover?

They felt all these issues would play a critical role in helping them decide what approach to take and the options that should be generated. They finally decided that taking a more positive approach would be most productive. In regard to income, they asked: How could they increase store revenue? Regarding staff they asked: How could they retain valuable staff members? Diane and Tim thought it wise to meet with the two Atlanta store department managers who helped conduct some of the employee and customer surveys and interviews.

The first thing they heard from Ben, the produce manager, was that he felt he got much wider and clearer information through the in-person interviews then when he just used the surveys. Since some of the information was gathered through just surveys and others were done with surveys first, in conjunction with follow-up interviews, the quality of the information varied.

Ben gave an example of his interview with Ron, an employee in his department, who felt like a lot of his time was being wasted.

When Ben was able to delve a little deeper into Ron's remarks, he found out that in one of the cases, Ron had to help unload trucks. Though this was part of his job, he felt his time was being wasted doing this particular job. However, in another instance, he mentioned always having to go to the assistant store manager before he could respond to all customer questions. Sometimes, he noted, he could have simply checked on an upcoming delivery list, so that also seemed a waste of time.

These were very different situations, and yet Ron was defining both as a waste of time. In the unloading the truck example, it was part of his job. However, in the customer question situation, there might be some way to make changes to resolve it, for instance find a different way to empower him and the other employees while also satisfying the customer.

As Tim and Diane discussed the information gathering process, they realized that the best information came when surveys were followed up with in-person interviews. Through this process, Tim and Diane could examine the survey responses and, in many cases, clarify what was meant by certain remarks. Finding out what was meant by some of the comments was very important in assessing exactly what respondents wanted to communicate.

After some preliminary investigation, where Tim and Diane canvassed the employees and customers, they realized that the shrinking number of customers had to do more with the expansion and recent increase in publicity and expanded hours for the new chain grocery in an adjacent community and was not directly due to a lower interest in coming to the Energize store.

During the in-person interviews Tim and Diane also observed that the respondents' body language did not always match up to the words they were saying. Some people said, "everything's fine," but had a scowl on their face as they said it. The scowl might have been related to the question and topic, but it might not have been. It was up to Tim and Diane as interviewers to assess if they should dig a little deeper by asking other follow-up questions.

As Tim and Diane got better at listening to not only what was being said, but also to what was not being said, new areas of inquiry opened up. One customer wrote down "more product information" on her survey. After Tim discussed it with her, he found out that the customer really wanted the store to offer more high-end products. Her feeling was that because of the store's emphasis on price, they were excluding some products that used more expensive ingredients or that were totally organic, because these would be priced higher.

From this experience, Tim and Diane realized that some customers had a hard time accurately putting their feelings into words and sometimes the words they used didn't exactly describe what they meant. Many times, as with this customer, Tim and Diane had to use their intuition, as when Diane assumed that because of the store's focus on offering low prices, they were ignoring more expensive products. In fact, Tim began thinking of proposing the creation a of pilot program to expand the store's product options, with no strong price restraints, by using customer input to define new possible offerings.

Restating/Reflecting has to do with taking the time to assess what we and others think, feel or believe. The act of restating what we have said, or what someone else has said, helps us consider how we're seeing and understanding a situation and whether others may be seeing it differently. This enables us to also explore why we and others affected by the problem may not think and feel the same way.

For instance, when the customer said she wanted more product information, by sitting down with her and clarifying what she meant, they were able to help the customer restate her comment. In doing so, they found that what she really meant was that she wished the store would expand its offerings.

Listening and observing more carefully, tuning into what's being said and to non-verbal clues (both ours and others'), and paying attention to our intuition—these are the crucial fundamentals in the restating/reflecting process.

After Tim and Diane completed their initial information and survey follow-up, they knew it was time to do a deep dive into the data they had. They knew that closely examining their deductions about what the information meant was critical. Tim and Diane had to use a more Inclusive/Reflective thinking approach by not only assessing the evidence but also by looking at how everyone involved felt about the issues.

Examination: Asking questions is the primary skill that is indispensable for the examination process. The types of questions we ask, and how we ask these questions, are both important elements at this stage, as they affect our interpretation of the information that we gather. It sounds easy, but it's not. It takes focus, serious effort, and being open-minded, but it's crucial before moving to the next step of confirming.

If possible, try to ask open-ended questions to ensure you are getting the best and most creative ideas, for example:

- Why do you think this situation exists?

- What if we think of a different way of doing it?

- How does the information we have connect with other information we're finding?

- What if we started with a blank page?

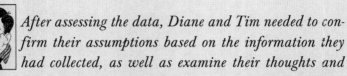

After assessing the data, Diane and Tim needed to confirm their assumptions based on the information they had collected, as well as examine their thoughts and feelings and those they'd gathered from others involved, before developing specific actions they planned to take. It was important for Diane and Tim to first delve into their own understanding of what the facts meant that came out of their interviews and survey information from customers and employees.

3. CONFIRM

After conducting our analysis and evaluation, we can now more thoughtfully decide if what we initially believed is true or whether our reasoning and evidence lead us to another view. To authenticate various beliefs, we need to look at why we believe something is true. Using reasoning and logic plays an important part in the Inclusive/Reflective thinking process as we judge the credibility of the evidence.

In analyzing and evaluating the proof of these arguments and facts, being aware of the pieces of information we're using to anchor our beliefs is crucial. We also cannot overlook our feelings about the situation. This will ultimately be an important element in our decision-making/problem-solving process and how we might go about moving to the next step.

 As they began to explore some of the facts uncovered, Diane and Tim needed to look at the context in which these played out so they could see if their beliefs were true. Some of the store's employee challenges were that many new people had been recently hired, which impeded the store's smooth operations. Digging deeper into these staffing issues, they were able to evaluate the evidence:

- *The assistant manager had left, and the new assistant manager didn't seem as competent.*
- *A long-term employee quit and the new person, being less knowledgeable, presented a challenge.*
- *One very flexible employee left and there seemed to not be much flexibility with the replacement.*
- *Another issue was they needed to assess the competition presented by the store that recently opened. This store was in close proximity and offered many of the same products and had more hours of operation.*

Belief to Truth

We must analyze and authenticate our beliefs. Many times, truth has to do with how a situation affects people. For example, if something helps me, I may believe it's good; if it harms me, I may see it as bad. How do we find the truth? It's important to look at various points of view. Assessing why we believe something and why others have their own beliefs, and considering the various contradictions, is crucial to the process.

In reasoning through the evidence and alleged facts, Diane and Tim explored the complaints from employees they received during their employee interviews about the lack of flexible working hours and inability to make more money.

Many of the employees were students and sometimes needed to adjust their schedules when the semesters changed. However, even when the switches seemed easy to do, they were hard to get implemented, as schedules were set at six-month intervals. Some of the employees also wanted to work more overtime when it was available, but it was usually assigned by seniority, even if those people weren't really interested in working the extra hours.

When Diane and Tim explored some of the other facts about the competition from the other store that opened nearby, they learned that the store was open late five nights a week (till 9 p.m.) and opened early at 8 a.m. three days. Since that store had changed its hours, the number of Energize customers had declined by 15%.

Using deductive reasoning, they felt pretty comfortable about their conclusion that the competing store's expanded hours might be playing a role in the Atlanta store losing customers. From customer surveys Diane and Tim found that most of the customers overwhelmingly requested that the store open earlier and close later at least some days. From that information, Diane and Tim were able to also inductively support their findings about sometimes opening the store earlier and closing it later.

However, since deductive reasoning is not always validated, they had to be sure about the correlation between the other store changing hours and Energizer's decline in customers was correct.

Giving Reasons and Evaluating Evidence

Reasoning through the proposed evidence using logic is essential. Unfortunately, not all evidence lends itself to a purely logical assessment when reviewing its credibility. The types of evidence we're using must be evaluated by thinking critically, which means having the ability to perceive and thoughtfully evaluate the conflicting realities. It involves the ability to draw the right conclusions from multiple data sources and assess the conclusions without bias, for the purpose of taking action. By taking the strength of that evidence into consideration, as well as any conflicting evidence, we will be able to assess all the possibilities and come up with our best thought-out interpretations. Deductive and inductive reasoning can often be helpful.

Deductive Reasoning is expressed as a series of connected premises, which leads to a conclusion. This type of reasoning starts from a general belief, which then leads to specific conclusions that follow the premises of that overall belief.

Inductive Reasoning is usually based on experience or observation. Inductive reasoning compares at least two events, ideas, or situations. The point of these comparisons is to establish whether these two sets under consideration are similar in a number of other ways and are also similar in a way that will support the claim that they are connected.

As Tim and Diane began to analyze and evaluate the information from the surveys and interviews, there were some things that seemed fairly obvious while others seemed less certain. Managers, like Tim, needing their stores to be profitable was an obvious fact, as their bonuses and ultimately their jobs depended on it. When it came to analyzing some of the new staff responses, they found that one of the employees had a serious argument with the new department manager and so his negative comments about the manager wasting his time had to be taken with that in mind. In addition, the fact that Tim and Diane were directly linking the other new store being open different hours to their decline in customers was not certain and had to be validated, which it later was.

Analyzing/Validating Data, Arguments and Interpretations

Using the classical method of evaluating the validity of information means that if your premise is true, and your argument is valid, then your proposition (conclusion) is sound.

With some arguments, we'll need more proof, especially if we're going against "conventional wisdom" or what seems obviously true to most people.

There is information that we tend to use as a guide or "anchor" which we attempt to compare with other data. We must also examine whether connecting elements are correctly linked as causation or just correlation. It is most important for us to examine how we're going about our evaluations and to be sure we're doing all we can to improve our interpretations.

"None of us is as smart as all of us."

— Ken Blanchard

---

4. CONSIDER OTHER POINTS OF VIEW (POV)

From what POV are you approaching the question, problem, or issue? Your POV enables you to see things in a certain light or perspective and is a filter, or lens, through which you organize your thinking. When thinking about POV, it is important to ask yourself what other POVs should you be considering with this issue—the boss's? the customer's? your subordinates?

 Diane and Tim knew that after they assessed all points of view—especially customers and employees—and had adequately confirmed their beliefs, the next step would be to make some definite decisions. They also knew that they'd have to reflect on both of their emotions and logic during their consideration.

"You cannot solve a problem

with the same level of thinking

that created it."

–Albert Einstein

REAL LIFE EXAMPLES:

Recall the problem that you were thinking of at the end of the last chapter—or if you prefer, think of a new problem you're facing on your job right now. As said previously, this could be a problem that has to do with customers, a product, a process, or even employee relations. However, it should be a real problem that affects others on your team as well as yourself. Use the questions below to help reflect on how you have explored the problem in order to define it more clearly:

- What do you believe is true about your situation? What evidence do you have?

- How do you/others think and feel about the situation?

- Why do you/others think and feel that way?

- How did you use inclusive and reflective thinking as you explored the problem?

- How have you taken both content and context into consideration in this situation?

- How have you practiced asking good questions and active listening regarding other people's point of view about the problem?

Step 4.
Generate, Analyze & Select Options

Brainstorming is a great technique to use to get new and novel options. It should be time focused, where participants are given an adequate amount of time for creative exploration. Before the session participants could be given time to think about what they'll be considering and come back with at least two or three options. This will insure the utmost participation.

There are also various brainstorming techniques such as brainwriting, the random word exercise, and others to consider. The important element is to help people think outside the box and not rely on tried and true answers or Automatic Thinking.

The most important guidelines about brainstorming sessions include:

- **Brainstorm without criticism**—in brainstorming, no idea should be judged good or bad.

- **Use possibility thinking**—a willingness to see possibilities everywhere instead of limitations.

At the conclusion of the brainstorming, the leader will guide a discussion that evaluates the ideas that came out of the session, in terms of which seem to work best, or most accurately address the problem. The person/s facing the problem should be the one/s who present the problem and guide the brainstorming. They also take the lead in the analyzing/selecting part of the session and serve as the ultimate decider of what option/s to select. Others in the group should challenge/question the leader to be sure they are objectively considering all options and not just going with their favorite or easy choice.

When sorting, ranking, developing and choosing options, be deliberate and explicit in creating choice criteria—for instance, if the problem is a need to get sales numbers up, expectations need to be defined about how much the sales numbers need to be up, and in what time period. Setting measurements for success will help us think more clearly and constructively about the factors that will influence the eventual success or failure of our efforts. Use individual criteria to select one or two high potential options to pursue for solving the problem.

DRAWING AND EXPLORING CONCLUSIONS

As we've seen, accurately identifying a problem requires us to stop and think, and then become aware of our own and others' possible biases, frames, and perspectives in defining the problem and possible solutions. In other words, we have to think it through, using Inclusive/Reflective thinking

Reaching sound conclusions using Inclusive/Reflective Thinking involves validating information and checking in with our intuition. For example, when Tim and Diane were looking at the problem, Tim felt it was similar to what he experienced in the past. Because of that, his intuition led him to think about using the same solution to this new situation. By overcoming his Automatic Thinking, he decided to include others' ideas to look at the situation in a much broader way.

This step gives you an opportunity to also troubleshoot for potential problems. When considering beliefs that result in actions, analytical thinking helps assess those actions—and more importantly, the consequences of those actions—before acting on those beliefs.

As you consider what will happen after you take the next steps in acting on your conclusions, you will need to develop a fuller, more complete understanding of the consequences of your actions. It's very important to realize that to accept a conclusion one must also accept its implications.

Before we have a response, another important aspect will be

for us to consider if the evidence points towards a need for us to look in other directions and should we then explore the other alternative possible conclusions they might lead us to.

DECISION-MAKING: TWO TYPES

As we look at decision-making, we'll see that the process for making decisions is not the same for every decision made. Some decisions require more time, energy and steps than others.

Indecision is sometimes
a failure to execute.

It's important to remember that creativity is critical in the generating phase, while careful analysis plays a big part in the analyzing and selecting phase of the problem-solving process.

Decision-making is often seen as a purely cognitive process, where the outcome is a logical choice between alternatives. And yet, frequently we make choices based on our "gut" feeling. However, our decision-making approach may fall somewhere in between thinking and feeling, and some people may have a preferred approach, just as people have different styles.

There are two basic types of decision-making:

- **Emotional decision-making** includes a whole range of decision-making processes, depending on the degree of logic that is included in the process.

- **Logical decision-making** uses only rational methods, including mathematical tools and metrics.

IMPORTANT:

Don't forget to include your
feelings when interpreting situations.

EMOTIONAL DECISION-MAKING

In making many decisions, we are sometimes more or less logical about them. A totally emotional decision typically comes very fast on the heels of identifying a problem. This is a reactive mode, and largely subconscious, i.e. decision-making that we encounter in heated arguments or when faced with immediate danger. These are also extreme examples of Automatic Thinking.

Good problem solvers realize that their feelings play an important part in their thinking and their responses to various situations. Rather than being ignored or treated as being irrelevant because they are "not logical," feelings need to be acknowledged, explored and incorporated in our response to a situation.

Good problem solvers also know that their feelings would be different if the outcome of their past experiences worked out in other ways. So, for instance, if the last time they worked with a specific person they felt they were taken advantage of, the next time they had to work with that same person, their feelings about their past experience would lead them to feel it would turn out the same way. Similarly, a good problem solver, if faced with having to solve a problem by laying off several people, would acknowledge their personal feelings about the individuals involved, whether they liked or disliked those individuals or had good or not-so-good interactions with them.

LOGICAL DECISION-MAKING

Logical decision-making is data-driven and based on a thoughtful analysis that compares the costs and benefits of an action. A logical decision-maker uses evidence and develops arguments and reasons to draw conclusions and make decisions. When we use logic to make decisions, we seek to minimize or even sometimes exclude emotions, using only rational methods.

For instance, when shopping for a new car, imagine that you see a practical model that has all the features you need at an affordable price. But then, across the showroom you see a hot new higher-priced red turbo-charged sports model with all the bells and whistles included. Some people would be tempted by the hot, red, unaffordable sporty model, simply because it's a car they'd always dreamed of driving, and they might even make the decision to buy it, based mainly on that emotion, that fantasy. Others would assess the situation more practically and logically, knowing they had to stay within their budget, but at the same time acknowledging their fantasy of driving around in a turbo-charged red sports car. They might even take it out for a spin—and then purchase the practical model that was within their budget.

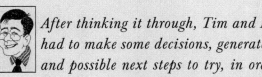 *After thinking it through, Tim and Diane knew they had to make some decisions, generate various options and possible next steps to try, in order to meet their challenges. They knew some new product offerings would probably make sense for their customers, and they felt they needed to create new avenues to help their employees make more money. In addition, they both guessed they would have*

> *to seriously consider opening the store two nights and two mornings a week, even on a trial basis, just to eliminate the risk of losing more customers while working to win back the ones who had already left.*

HAVING A RESPONSE

When we are satisfied that we have adequately generated and analyzed options for solving the problem at hand, it's time to select the option(s) that will give us the greatest reward for the resources we'll be investing. The most important point is that the solution must be doable. It could also be a series of solutions. However, the series needs to be sequentially organized to have the best results. So, for instance, if we decide to meet with the staff, survey the customers and check out the competition, we'll first have to organize how the steps will be completed and in what order.

After using the Thinking It Through Process we have outlined, our response will be more thoughtful and fully explored. The subsequent result of what we do and say will then often be a more successful outcome.

However, sometimes we will also see that taking NO action, or waiting for a more opportune time, might be the most appropriate response. An example would be when Diane decided not to move on the first answer she came up with, but instead waited and took the time to work with Tim to explore the problem further.

> ## "The outcome of any judgment is based on who judges and not what's being judged."
>
> —Krishna

NEXT STEPS

As we move to creating and implementing a plan, there are some other questions for us to consider.

Examples:

- How do we determine if we need to wait for a more opportune time?

- Do we need more information or time? If so, how can we get the information or time we need?

- Do we need other people's input? How can we get those other people involved?

- How might we take action?

- As we begin to figure all this out, are there other areas we need to explore?

As you complete these final steps, you will see that logic and reason play a vital part in analyzing and evaluating the data collected through using Inclusive/Reflective Thinking as part of the Thinking It Through Process. The goal is for us to be able to make decisions using the most accurate interpretations of the problem, which will help us be sure we're assessing and generating our best solutions.

REAL LIFE EXAMPLES

Think of the problem you're facing on your job right now that you focused on in the last chapter. Remind yourself of who was involved and your awareness of your own and others' perspectives on the problem, and what you did to investigate alternate definitions of the problem and possible solutions proposed by both others and yourself.

- What conclusions have you come to? How did you come to those conclusions?

- How have you creatively generated options to your problem?

- How did you select the best option to pursue?

- If you've made any decisions, what processes have you used in your decision-making?

- What part, if any, have emotion and logic played in the generating ideas about the problem and possible solutions?

- What possible solutions did you consider before selecting the best possible one/s?

"By failing to prepare

you are preparing to fail."

— Benjamin Franklin

Step 5:
Implement Solutions
Step 6:
Review & Assess Progress

I n being more inclusive and taking time to stop and think through each phase of the problem-solving process, we adequately collected, clarified and confirmed what we thought was true, as well as considered other points of view. These are critical parts of the process.

The previous section helped us generate, analyze and select options. In this section, we'll now explore how we can implement solutions by first of all fully assessing our current environment. We also need to create a plan which includes how to get the proper support to accomplish our goals. Understanding our strengths and weaknesses and what we can personally contribute will be crucial in helping us to move forward. Using effective communication is also a critical component to our success.

Lastly, we'll cover how we can Review and Assess Progress at the end of this section. There's no way to really know for sure that our solutions are working until we can check our progress against measurable outcomes.

ASSESSING THE ENVIRONMENT
USING SITUATIONAL ANALYSIS

In order to pull all our thinking together before taking Step 5—Implementing Solutions—it's essential for us to do a Situational Analysis. Basically, this is the process of critically evaluating the internal and external conditions for you and your organization, which are relevant to the problem. A Situational Analysis is done prior to implementing a new initiative or project. This provides the knowledge to identify the current opportunities and challenges to your organization, service or product. We do this to assess the environment we're working in before moving forward.

ACKNOWLEDGEMENT

Ask yourself:

- What am I focusing on?

- What is my interpretation of the current problem?

- What lens am I using to see the problem?

- How might I be framing the problem?

As an example, in creating a new project, your responses might be:

- I'm focusing on the cost.

- My interpretation is it's going to be very costly.

- I've already spent a good amount of time and money preparing.

- I'm just framing it from a financial point of view

That's your interpretation of the problem, including your acknowledgement of your own point of view. And then ask yourself how other people might be seeing the problem differently than you. The fact that other people may have different views about the problem will help you understand that there may be additional truths you might want to consider.

AWARENESS

As ironic as it sounds, you must somehow learn to take the most objective look at your subjective view. Step outside of yourself and see what else is going on regarding the situation and the problem. This consists of taking two views:

Micro view: How does the way you're viewing it differ from others' views? How are you and others feeling about this problem? Why do you think that is? What's the specific atmosphere regarding the situation, i.e. the people involved, their roles, the time allowed to explore the problem, and any other environmental aspects, for you and others involved with the situation, right here, right now.

Macro view: Next take a wider view. What is the general atmosphere surrounding the situation? What other things are going on with you and those involved in the immediate environment and even beyond, now and in the future, that may affect the situation and how you and others are viewing this?

With both views, look at what information you have and what other information you might need to acquire.

ACCEPTANCE

The previous steps lead to this final stage. What does all this mean? What's reality? How can we deal with all the outside noise—the thoughts and feelings about the situation, yours and others' evaluation/judgment of it, whether good or bad, important or unimportant?

Taking these steps will help you form your most objective view. Knowing and understanding the space you're in—the people involved, outside factors affecting the problem—will help you now to move forward and organize and implement your best response.

Although Tim and Diane felt confident about their decisions as they moved forward, they knew it would be good to step back and take as objective a view as possible. It would be important to acknowledge their current interpretation of the situation, have total awareness of the other possible ways of seeing it and accept everything else surrounding the situation that might affect their view.

Employee turnover: *Tim and Diane decided to set up a pilot bonus program where employees who were able to get extra sales on the higher-end products would share in the profits that were generated. They would also set up a new flex-time employee work schedule where employees who wanted to shift their schedule could apply for a change of schedule and other employees could opt to fill in their schedules by taking those spots and have the opportunity to make additional money.*

By both creating an opportunity for employees to make more money and setting up a more flexible work schedule, Tim and Diane thought this would help decrease turnover and cut down on overtime among employees.

Store's decline in profits, loss of customers, and store hours: *Diane and Tim decided that they would experiment with having the store stay open late, till 9 p.m. two nights a week and by having it open early two days a week at 8 a.m. instead of 9 a.m.*

To address other customer concerns, Diane and Tim came up with an idea to create a high-end product order system where those products could be ordered in advance by the customers.

Diane and Tim also came up with a bonus program for customer loyalty. If a customer spent over $450 a month on their store credit card, they would receive a $15 coupon for purchases the following month. This was tried successfully in the Florida Energize store a year before.

Another project they thought of was to have a member of the management team visit the competitor once a week, fill out a survey form and report back on their findings. Tim and Diane would evaluate the results of their proposals two months later and make adjustments based on the findings.

Diane realized that Tim had many of the skills necessary to carry out the plan. He was very organized and detail-oriented. Where Tim's skills needed improvement, his communication skills, she would offer to send him to training. She also made sure that Tim knew that she would be there herself to help him get the proper tools and other resources to support him in being successful.

STEP 5. IMPLEMENT SOLUTIONS

Your job in Step 5 is to create an implementation plan. The real first steps, however, include last-minute questions such as: Do we need more research? Should we involve other people? When, where, and how do we do that? Am I the right person to make this happen?

This is where your ideas become reality. In creating an implementation plan, you should record tasks to be done, time frames when work needs to be completed and/or reports filed, and who will be responsible for each task. People's skills and abilities, as well as their availability, are important factors when deciding on assignments and deadlines. This aspect of putting your team together is critical at this stage. Think about the stakeholders who will be affected by your plan and those who will be responsible for approving or rejecting your initiative. Especially crucial are those team members who you need to actively assist you in bringing your ideas to fruition.

The time frames should be realistic, and alternative plans might be formulated, should unforeseen circumstances arise. Deadlines might be tied to regular weekly or monthly meetings, quarterly reports, or other typical cycles that happen within the organization.

Another important aspect of this step is assessing potential obstacles. This will give you a chance to think them through before they happen, and come up with ideas of how you might overcome them, if they do happen. An example would be if Diane thought that upper management might balk at the expense of having the store open additional hours. In that case, she would have to come up with a plan that would take that into consideration and make it financially viable or at least a good investment in the eyes of management and those making decisions about budgets.

FOCUS ON YOUR STRENGTHS

Truly knowing yourself, both your strengths and weaknesses, is critical to your success. What are your special gifts and talents? We all have them, although some of us have a hard time identifying them. If you have truly applied yourself in Step 1, in developing an awareness of yourself and your POV, your frames and your experiences which influence your thinking, you should be ready to take this next step.

We also have weaknesses. Either working on those limitations or joining with others who have strengths in those areas will help you move forward. It's knowing how to contribute that will help you have greater success.

Working together, Diane and Tim got to know their own strengths and weaknesses. They also had a good idea about what support they had in the Atlanta store and what support they might expect from the company, as they proceeded to implement their solutions to the problems they had explored. Tim knew a couple of his senior staff had the knowledge and skills to assist him in working with the more junior staff to help them in implementing the planned changes. Diane also knew that Paul and the other senior managers would help give her feedback, ideas and support as she worked with Tim to ensure his success.

SUPPORT

It is important that in moving forward we also have support in the form of a sounding board, or someone who can help us by giving objective feedback and guidance. There are a number of ways for us to get support in either a group or individual setting. Some possibilities are:

Mentors: Mentoring is a relationship between someone with potential and an individual with expertise. It could be either a formal and an informal relationship. Either way, the goal should be to transmit knowledge, social capital, and/or social support perceived by the recipient as relevant to work, career, or professional development.

Affinity Groups: Affinity groups, also called networking groups, provide forums for individuals or employees to gather socially and share ideas outside of their particular environment or business units.

Mastermind Groups: A mastermind group is a peer-to-peer mentoring group used to help members solve their problems with input and advice from the other group members. The concept was originated by author Napolean Hill in 1925 and has grown and evolved to become a staple tool for many successful individuals.

Diane and Tim gave Paul a call back in the home office, to get his advice on what support they thought the company could supply. Diane thought she might use the Manager's group to test their ideas and get support.

As part of the process, Diane had to take their plan to Paul for his approval. Paul appreciated the effort Diane and Tim had put into the plan. They had collected and evaluated important information, clarifying its authenticity and confirming their final conclusions through a methodical and complete system of thinking.

Paul developed his pitch to the group of VPs who needed to sign off on it. He knew that he'd need to show his enthusiasm and also use a persuasive line of reasoning to win them over. Ultimately, he let the VPs know that if the Atlanta store was able to increase its profitability, it would positively affect the VPs' bonuses.

Although there was some monetary investment required for the proposal, Paul felt that many of the concepts that would be implemented could be used as pilot projects for other stores to replicate throughout the system.

Their project was approved unanimously by the executive committee at their March meeting. After that success, Paul, Diane and Tim planned a major celebration dinner for their June regional meeting.

STEP 6. REVIEW AND ASSESS PROGRESS

Reviewing progress is a critical aspect to implementing a successful plan. As you assess the progress of your solutions towards solving the problem you had originally encountered, you will learn what's working and not working. It's very important to set up multiple progress reviews, where the timing and number of reviews will be crucial.

Progress reviews allow you to identify any course corrections needed to be sure you're moving in the right direction. These modifications will then have to be carefully planned out and observed for their effectiveness.

Many times, there are natural points in the process, like getting approval or funding during the plan, that can provide you an opportunity for review. There could also be metrics that you are using to gauge success—sales numbers increasing or errors decreasing—which will allow you an opportunity for assessment. If this doesn't exist in your plan, you should try to create a break early in the process to take a hard look at your progress.

Creating a way to capture what you learn will be essential in helping you improve your current project and make better future plans.

Be sure to get multiple perspectives on the data you're collecting and how it's being analyzed in order to get the widest and most accurate information.

EFFECTIVE COMMUNICATION

Diane remembers when she first worked with Tim and was trying to get him focused on managing his inventory more effectively. Although she thought she was being clear, Tim misinterpreted her message and automatically

> *increased his inventory rather than analyzing his current stock. Diane and Tim subsequently realized that they had to set up an effective communication system to be sure their plan was understood clearly, carried out effectively, and that everyone had a chance to give input and ask any questions they had.*

The most critical element in effectively implementing your plans to solve any problem is communication. How well you communicate with those involved in your situation will prove to be a key to success.

Communication is about getting your message across to others clearly and unambiguously, as well as taking the time to listen and understand their messages to you. The important elements of communication include:

- the message itself,

- the person sending it,

- the person/s receiving it,

- the context—the who, what, when, where, how, and why that gives the message its meaning.

Remember:

Everyone wants to be heard and understood.

You also need to give those you're working with as many opportunities as possible to give you feedback. Your team will provide verbal and nonverbal reactions as feedback to your communicated message. Pay close attention to this feedback, as it is something important that allows you to verify whether or not your audience—the recipient of your message—has understood your message and you have received their input.

If you find that there has been a misunderstanding, at least you'll have the opportunity to correct it. A misunderstanding, however, may be another opportunity to get new ideas or obtain different views that could possibly make your ideas better. Remember to give feedback, too, so that everyone involved knows how things are progressing and how they're doing.

REAL LIFE EXAMPLES

Think back on the problem you've been prompted to think of at the end of each chapter. In this final section, think about the ways you'll be able to assess whether or not the solutions to your problem can be adequately planned for and how will you assess its success.

- How will you effectively plan the next steps to take in order to implement and assess your problem-solving project?

- How will you assess the environment and context of the problem and possible solutions?

- What ways will you use to assess and utilize your strengths?

- What are the ways you'll communicate and develop ongoing support?

Summary
The Six Steps

The Six Step Problem Solving model can be used as a whole process, employing all six steps to address and solve a problem in the workplace—or outside the workplace, for that matter. Alternately, parts of the process can be applied, depending upon the situation and the time available. However, an awareness of various points of view and biases (Step 1) and being able to define the true problem (Step 2) and clearly think the problem through (Step 3) are pretty much essential elements to all problem-solving efforts.

Before you begin to work on solving any problem, Stop & Think! There are always some good questions you should ask to launch the process:

- Is a solution possible?

- Is this the right time to be considering this?

- What if we wait or do nothing?

- Do we need others to supply information and/or help to come up with a solution?

- If so, are these other people available to work on this problem?

STEP 1. DEVELOP AWARENESS (INVESTIGATE)

Use questioning techniques to learn what you and others think and feel about a particular issue. Help develop and think through ideas as a prelude to evaluating them. When confronted with a new idea, you want to understand it, relate it to your experience, and determine its implications, consequences, and value. By doing this you can effectively uncover the structure of your own and others' perspectives.

Asking probing questions are a means to achieve your goals. It's also important to become comfortable being asked questions. Try not to become offended, confused, or intimidated when someone questions your description of a problem or suggestions for solutions. Don't confuse being questioned with being criticized. Welcome good questions as an opportunity to develop and refine your own line of thinking.

Step 1 is all about investigating. Those who have information about the problem should explain the important elements of it to team members. Others who are involved in the problem-solving effort should ask key questions to get other needed data to further understand the problem, for instance:

- What is specifically happening or not happening?

- What do you know about this? How do you feel about it?

- What don't you know about this?

- How do others involved think and feel about this?

- What's helping it continue to occur?

- What's preventing it from getting fixed?

- What would the best scenario look like?

- What else is going on that might affect this?

STEP 2. DEFINE THE PROBLEM (DETERMINE)

At least 50% of problem exploration involves being able to critically identify the question you begin with. Formulate the problem—the issue, the challenge—as a question clearly and precisely to define exactly what you want to explore in order to answer or solve the problem. This is a crucial element for the problem-solving process. It's a step that will help you get to the heart of the problem by formulating the right questions, for instance:

- Where, when and with whom is the problem occurring?
- How and why is the problem happening?
- What are the critical elements, issues and unique features of the situation?
- What are the certainties and uncertainties associated with this problem?
- What are the risks and consequences of the problem?
- What is your role and how does this problem affect you?
- How do others view the problem?
- Who should be involved in solving the problem?

Finally, try to define the problem in the form of an open-ended question, one that can't be answered with a "yes" or "no" or a one-word response, i.e. How will we ...?

STEP 3. EXPLORE THE PROBLEM (EXAMINE)

This next stage is to research the problem as fully as possible, using the Thinking it Through Process of Inclusive/Reflective Thinking.

Collect and Assess Information:
- What data (a) are we using or (b) do we need to get to support or clarify our beliefs?

- What other information will we need to know? Is it available? Will it be credible?

Clarify/Recognize/Explore Assumptions & Evaluate Evidence:

- What beliefs, attitudes, feelings, ideas are we taking for granted?

- What is our evidence and how solid is it? Are there other assumptions we can make?

Confirm/Explore Conclusions/Consequences/ Implications:

- What conclusions can we reach as a result of assessing those assumptions?

- What are the possible implications/consequences as a result of these conclusions?

Consider Other Points of View:

- From which point(s) of view are we considering this issue?

- What other perspectives should we be considering?

STEP 4. GENERATE, ANALYZE & SELECT OPTIONS (EXPAND & DECIDE)

Generating:

Brainstorming is the most effective tool for generating ideas, whether that means ideas for solving a problem in the workplace—or even ideas for solving challenges in our personal or social lives. And, although brainstorming is seen as a kind of freewheeling, "anything goes" process, it only works if you follow certain guidelines to define and give structure to the process. At the conclusion of the brainstorming activity, the leader can prioritize the options presented, based on which might be the most workable.

Analyzing and Selecting:
When analyzing the various options for solving the problem, in order to select a solution that seems to be the best route to take, the most important questions to consider are:

- Is it doable?

- What is good/bad about this idea?

- What is liked/disliked about the idea?

- What will give you the greatest return for the amount of resources you'll be investing?

- Which options for solving the problem might lend themselves to gauging progress?

STEP 5. IMPLEMENT SOLUTIONS (TAKE ACTION)

A plan of action to solve the problem should contain specific tasks, dates, and people responsible for implementation. Identifying those tasks, dates, and people involves asking some additional questions, for instance:

- Do we need research?

- Do we the have the right people to implement this solution?

- Should we be involving other people and when, where, and how do we do that?

Communicate the plan face-to-face with those who will be involved in implementing it. An important aspect of this step is setting up processes for ongoing observation, review, and feedback from those involved. Through this feedback you will be able to look ahead to anticipate potential obstacles, which gives you the ability to come up with ideas about how you might overcome them. Anticipating roadblocks ahead gives you the ability to take an alternate route or remove the roadblocks. Being aware that there may, indeed, be roadblocks ahead is critical for your plan's success.

Questions for putting an effective team together:
- Who do I need on my team? How will I get them to participate?

- Am I the right person to lead this solution effort?

- What objections, difficulties and obstacles might there be? How might I overcome them?

- What might I do to gain acceptance?

Questions most important to consider:
- What will the situation look like when the problem is solved?

- What is the very first thing we need to do?

- Who should be doing it?

- When can each task be done?

- What resources will you need in terms of people, money, and facilities?

STEP 6. REVIEW AND ASSESS PROGRESS (EVALUATE)

Put together a team and create a process for how and when you will review the progress of your plan. Specific dates should be set for these reviews. Initial reviews need to be done early in the process to be sure course corrections can be created and implemented, if needed. Throughout the implementation process, there are likely natural points to schedule reviews, such as getting approval for funding or quarterly sales reports. Creating a plan to collect and assess what you're learning as the plan unfolds will give you feedback both on how things are progressing—or not—and how you might improve future plans.

Most important questions for measuring success:
- How can we set up a time and a process to review progress?

- What will we do if the plan is not being followed or working out as expected?

- How will we create a way to capture what's being learned?

"Listen carefully and

learn continuously."

—Marshall Goldsmith

CONCLUSION

After taking the journey through this book, we hope that your Inclusive/Reflective thinking skills have improved. At times, taking the Automatic Thinking route is adequate for solving routine problems. However, on many occasions, it is essential to take more time and use the Thinking It Through process.

If you follow this Six Step process, you will be able to become more thoughtful and a better problem solver, as you take the time to stop and think before you proceed. Taking the time to move through the steps of collecting, clarifying and confirming the information you need, while considering other points of view, will help you to be sure you're asking all the right questions and more fully examining the many possibilities for defining and solving a problem. Using Inclusive/Reflective thinking will also provide you with the ability to explore your situation from various perspectives, which frequently opens up a variety of possibilities that would not exist if you were just using Automatic Thinking.

When you are effectively and efficiently using the techniques and tools we've outlined throughout the book, you'll find you don't have to use every element of each step in all the problems you face in the workplace and elsewhere. Use your available time wisely, by picking and choosing the components that will work best for you in your particular situation.

Even outside the workplace, by using the information in this book, you will become a master thinker, able to make better decisions and create the right solutions to your problems in ways that will last and make your investment of time well spent.

Become an Essential Problem Solver. Always remember to Stop & Think!

Everything is
Situational.

The Six Steps
Real Life Example

Paul remembers when he first came to Energize. It was an important time in his career when he was a regional manager. Soon after becoming a manager, Paul decided to pursue his idea about increasing the viability of using more local organic produce for the Energize stores in his region. He applied to the company's Innovation Awards program and his idea was selected as one of four to receive a grant. Those who received a grant had to submit a proposal by the end of the year.

Paul knew that other competing companies were focusing more in the direction of organic and local products and that the Energize marketing VP was a big proponent of organic as well.

The important issues for the project's success were to assemble the team and get the plan done by year end. Although Paul thought that it may take more money to fund the research needed than the $5,000 grant he received, he thought he might be able to get some additional funding from other sources.

The first step Paul thought was to explore how he would assemble the resources to complete the plan.

On the following pages is an outline of how the process worked. His approach was to develop awareness about the issue and then describe the challenge in the form of an open-ended question.

STOP & THINK—INITIAL PRELIMINARY QUESTIONS:

- Is this the right time to be considering this? Is it time sensitive?
  Paul had to get the proposed plan in by the end of the year.

- Are others needed to supply information and/or help to come up with a good solution?
  Yes, research was needed, which would include many other points of view on the issue.

STEP 1. INVESTIGATE

- What is known about this problem?
  Paul knows that many competing stores are focusing on organic and local. Also, a number of Energize executives on the committee that will approve the plan believe this is an important direction the company should be going in.

- What isn't known about this?
  Paul isn't certain what the consequences might be of pursuing this initiative.

- Why is this happening?
  More customers are asking for organic and more competing companies are offering it.

- How does Paul and others think and feel about this problem?
  Paul thinks this issue is very important to the company's future success, but he's not sure if many of the key people in the company feel it's important, so he's not sure how much direct support there would be from others in the company.

- What's preventing it from getting fixed or happening?
  It requires an investment of time and money. Most people seem busy with other projects.

- What would the best scenario look like?
  The proposed plan gets submitted within the time frame and accepted by the executive committee.

- What else is going on that might affect this?
  Two other new projects are being started in Paul's department involving some of the same people he would need to assist him.

STEP 2. DETERMINE

- Define the problem in the form of an open-ended question.
  Paul asked: How can we get the resources needed to effectively implement this plan?

- Revise the version of your question after clarifying the concepts in the question.
  Paul revised his question to include a definition of "resources": How can we get the needed funds and people to effectively implement this plan on time and on budget?

STEP 3. EXAMINE

COLLECT & ASSESS INFORMATION

Information:
- Paul knows he currently has a $5,000 budget for the project, from the grant he received.

- Paul's knows the proposal has to be completed by the end of the year.

- Paul needs to explore if he'll need more money to accomplish the research needed.

Evaluating Credibility:

- Paul needs to check with his boss to see if there are budget areas in the department that he can apply to if he needs additional money.

- Paul knows that the time for the plan submission is locked in.

- Paul needs to get an estimate for the research he'll need.

CLARIFY, RECOGNIZE & CHALLENGE ASSUMPTIONS

Assumption 1: Paul would have trouble getting additional funding for his project.
Evidence 1: Paul had been told by his boss that the department budget is set and other people in his department have not received funding for new projects.

Assumption 2: Paul would have trouble getting people involved in his project.
Evidence 2: Paul's department's staff told him that they're stretched too thin, and no new projects in his department have been started this year.

CONFIRM & EXPLORE CONCLUSIONS, CONSEQUENCES, IMPLICATIONS

Conclusion 1: If Paul needs extra funding, he won't be able to get funding from his department's budget.
Consequence/Inference 1: Paul needs to think about new possibilities for getting money.

Conclusion 2: It might be hard for Paul to get people from his department to work on this project.
Consequence/Inference 2: Paul would need to go outside his department to get people from other departments to assist him or hire new outside people.

CONSIDER OTHER POINTS OF VIEW

Paul believes this is a very worthwhile issue for Energize to pursue.

- Paul believes other people in the department feel overwhelmed and he's not sure they think the organic/local issue is very important.
  Paul will have to check in with other people in his department.

- Paul isn't sure his boss sees this issue as a big priority for the company to pursue.
  Paul will have to meet with his boss to discuss this issue and try to get her support.

STEP 4. EXPAND & DECIDE

GENERATE OPTIONS

After brainstorming with some of his peers, Paul and a number of his colleagues came up with a few options they thought would work:

- Create a multi-department team.

- Identify other potential sources for funding and help.

- Get Paul's boss and other highly placed Energize executives involved.

EVALUATE AND SELECT SOLUTIONS

Paul finally decided on three specific solutions to pursue:

- Get his boss involved immediately, since her support was important for approval of the project.

- Send out project information to other department heads to get them involved and willing to provide support, possible research and/or funding assistance.

- Put a cross-functional team from these various departments together to provide adequate assistance.

STEP 5. TAKE ACTION

Paul then created a three-month plan to implement the selected solutions:

What	Who	When
Get an invitation out to some colleagues about the proposal	Paul	1/19
Brainstorm with some colleagues	Paul, John, Mary	1/26
Create/Send Paul's boss an outline of his proposed idea	Paul	2/1
Meet with his boss at his weekly scheduled meeting to pitch his idea	Paul & Bill	2/09
Create an information package	Paul/his team	3/16
Send out the information package	Paul's assistant	3/22
Select potential team members and assign tasks	Paul and team	3/28
Finalize an estimate of research that will be needed	Team members	4/7
Review progress	Paul	4/13
Set a cross-department team meeting	Paul/respondents	4/22

STEP 6. EVALUATE

What	Who	When
Put together a group to review progress	Paul	4/13
Set dates to review progress with the team	Paul & team	4/15
Create a way to capture learnings	Paul & team	4/17

SUMMARY

As planned, Paul went together with Bill to meet with his boss and they were able to get her approval and support for the project. Paul next put together his team to create a plan for collecting the needed research. The team also created an information package and recruited other team members to assist in implementing the plan, reviewing progress and capturing what they'd learned.

Though he did encounter a few objections and bumps along the way, ultimately Paul achieved his goal. He secured enough funding from other departments to supplement his grant to carry out the research needed for his idea of having Energize expand their offerings of local organic produce. The end result of the research was that it seemed like a viable idea. Most importantly, he met the deadline for submitting his proposal by the end of the year.

Paul used the Six Step model again when he built into the roll-out plan ways to capture and evaluate progress. The company needed to know if it was working—i.e. if customers were aware of the new produce offerings, and if so, what were their reactions. Paul's evaluation plan included gathering information from store managers, customers and employees about their experiences and reactions to the new produce offerings. Of course, Paul also had to demonstrate with hard numbers that adding local organic produce was a worthwhile effort for Energize. We're happy to report that he was able to show that the new produce offerings were a financial success.

"The beginning of wisdom is
the knowledge of your own ignorance."

— Benjamin Franklin

"My way toward the truth
is to ask the right questions."

— Socrates

How I Became a Problem-Solving Guide and an Inclusive/Reflective Thinker

I have made many big and small decisions in solving problems throughout my life, both personally and professionally. What I have noticed is that using Inclusive/Reflective thinking—using both the logical and emotional sides of my brain—and taking the time to think over some of those major decisions has made a critical difference, especially in my career choices.

My career began on Wall Street, where I worked my way up from a low-level runner, through many back-office jobs, to become a high-level trader—a good position to be in for a young man in his mid-twenties, with no college under his belt and no real business connections.

Although all the essential elements seemed to be in place for a successful well-paid career, it seemed to me something was missing. At the time, I was also doing volunteer work as a Big Brother. Even though I enjoyed volunteering, the feeling that I wasn't really doing anything meaningful in my work life kept coming up. At lunches and company functions with my peers, when the topic turned to important issues that were going on in our lives, it seemed the most common areas discussed were how much money people were making and/or the size of their expense account.

Since that didn't feel satisfying to me, after giving it some serious thought, I hatched a plan to leave my job, equip a van for a cross-country trip and eventually settle on the West Coast. There I attended college to figure out my future. This was a major decision that wasn't based on what seemed logical to many others, but to me it felt right. I believe this event set the stage for what would become the inclusive/reflective way I would consider most major problems in my life.

Several years later, I was working as an account executive at a recruiting firm where I had just become a department supervisor. The branch manager had taken me under his wing and was grooming me to take over his job. At the same time, I had made a connection with a local nonprofit agency and helped them get a small grant for a student learning program. After that, I wasn't involved with the nonprofit for a while, but since I was with a recruiting firm, one day out of the blue, they contacted me. Their Executive Director was retiring, and they needed some help replacing her. It took me only a short time to decide that I was, in fact, the perfect candidate.

When this opportunity came to me, I had just been promoted, I was making a good salary and I was at the front of the line to take over as office manager. As I pondered the Executive Director position, I thought it would be a perfect opportunity for me. Did this decision make logical sense? The nonprofit job paid less and was a total gamble, but still, I felt strongly it would be my best move. Of course, when I was finally offered the job, I jumped at it. In making this decision I wondered if I was ignoring logic to make a heart-over-head decision once again.

When I left that job, which I held for 17 years, it made perfect sense to just get another senior nonprofit management position. However, after taking some time to reflect on my choices, I again rolled the dice and, instead of making the logical decision, I decided to start my own consulting/training company. Although my training experience wasn't overwhelming, I felt confident enough that my Executive Director background would provide me with many of the skills I'd need as a consultant/trainer.

In solving this big problem of how I would make a living, after taking the time to reflect, I could see that once again it seemed as if I overruled the "logical" choice and used my intuition and feelings to make my decision to start my own business.

As I look back now, I can see why I am so attracted to using both my logic and my intuition—inclusive and reflective thinking, which is the cornerstone of my training in the essentials of problem solving.

This book represents many years of business experience as well as my experiences consulting, training, and coaching. In creating this model there have been many iterations which I have fine-tuned over years of working with clients in many different sectors. I developed the Six Step Problem Solving Method, built on the foundations of Inclusive/Reflective thinking, in the hope that it will serve you as well in making decisions and solving problems, as you move forward in business and in life.

About Results for Change

Results for Change offers training, coaching, and consulting for helping organizations enhance and improve employee engagement by giving them the tools they need to make better decisions, solve problems, and get optimum results.

Results for Change offers lively, interactive, motivating, hands-on courses that help create solutions to real problems in areas essential for business success. Sessions are developed to incorporate real life business situations particular to the company or industry. Participants get the chance to practice with their case examples using the tools presented from each module of this book. Through these team interactions, learning is integrated throughout the entire group.

It is our goal for you to be successful in solving your problems. Toward that end, we also want to offer you a chance to work with us at Results for Change in either a group or individual setting. If you're interested in getting more information about the options available, please get in touch.

We also want to learn from you. Let us know your experiences in applying these tools and using Inclusive/Reflective thinking to solve your real-life problems in the workplace. By sharing our knowledge and experiences we all become better Essential Problem Solvers.

For more information:
www.resultsforchange.org
914-690-9200

Acknowledgments

There is a question I am always interested in asking: "How can we use our best collective thinking to come up with solutions that last?" I've been working on the answer to that for many years now.

There have been many people who have influenced me with their thinking and ideas. Initially, Dr. Karl Albrecht, who I met through my work with the American Management Association, introduced me to the concept of thinking styles, which sparked my interest in "thinking about thinking."

I have also been influenced by ideas and readings from many thought leaders such as Chris Argyris, Stephen Covey, Howard Gardner, Marshall Goldsmith, Guy Claxton, Edward DeBono, Linda Elder, Tim Hurson, John Maxwell, Daniel Kahneman, Ken Blanchard and Malcolm Gladwell.

As my thinking began to take shape and I narrowed it down to what became the main elements in this book, a number of people helped clarify my ideas. I feel honored to have many wonderful people in my life, both friends and those I've had the opportunity to work together with.

A special thanks goes to Rich Spitz, who stuck with me through thick and thin and played a key role by giving me constant feedback as he suffered through the first draft of this book. Also, my late friend Richard Manley provided the graphic of Paul, and was a constant commenter when I first constructed my concept.

Many thanks as well to Dawn Daisley of MorningLiteBook-Designs, who went above and beyond in creating the graphics and beautiful layout. Finally, to my editor, Margaret Daisley of Blue Horizon Books, who provided incredible insight and ideas. Without her help this book would not have been completed.

Nothing can be created without love and support, and so my thanks would not be complete without acknowledging my wife Linda who provided me those attributes and more as I struggled over the years to get my manuscript finalized.

I wrote this book because I wanted to help people learn how to solve problems in a more efficient and effective way. So lastly, I want to acknowledge you, my readers, for joining me on this journey.

> **"There is no limit to what can be accomplished if it doesn't matter who gets the credit."**
>
> —Ralph Waldo Emerson

Index

Standing still is sometimes one of the best steps

we can take in the dance of life.

Made in the USA
Middletown, DE
26 June 2021